COMMUNITY, CULTURE, AND ECONOMIC DEVELOPMENT

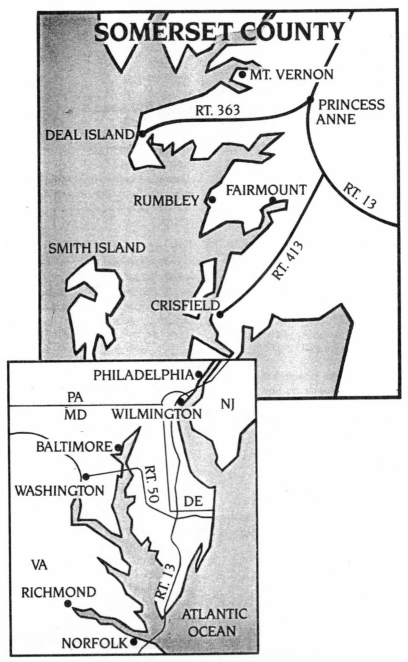

Map of Somerset County, Maryland

COMMUNITY, CULTURE, AND ECONOMIC DEVELOPMENT

The Social Roots of Local Action

MEREDITH RAMSAY

STATE UNIVERSITY OF NEW YORK PRESS

SUNY Series, Democracy in American Politics
David J. Vogler, Editor

Published by
State University of New York Press, Albany

© 1996 State University of New York

For information, address State University of New York
Press, State University Plaza, Albany, N.Y., 12246

Production by E. Moore
Marketing by Dana E. Yanulavich

Library of Congress Cataloging-in-Publication Data

Ramsay, Meredith, date
    Community, culture, and economic development : the social roots of
local action / Meredith Ramsay.
        p.   cm. — (SUNY series, democracy in American politics)
    Includes bibliographical references and index.
        ISBN 0-7914-2749-8 (alk. paper). — ISBN 0-7914-2750-1 (pbk. :
alk. paper)
        1. Community development—Maryland—Somerset County.
    2. Economic development—Social aspects—Maryland—Somerset
County. 3. Social action—Maryland—Somerset County. I. Title.
II. Series.
HN79.M32S67   1995
338.9752'23—dc20   95-4241
                                                                                  CIP

Contents

LIST OF FIGURES

PREFACE

This book is based upon research that I carried out as a doctoral student in political science. It presents a history of how two different communities in Somerset County, Maryland, have responded to economic change and other disturbing events. Once I began the field research for this project, it did not take long for me to discover that my uninvited presence in this isolated rural county was itself a disturbing event. Hence the nature of my encounters with the people there became part of the data.

I am a white woman. Whether this worked to my advantage or to my disadvantage, I cannot say. It is certain, however, that my race, class, sex, and southern background—and my status as an outsider—profoundly affected the ways in which people in Princess Anne and Crisfield responded to me and I to them. The character of these interactions gave me a great deal of insight into the traditional culture and social structures that I went there to study, so I believe that it is important for me to share some of my personal experiences with the reader. I hope that this will be of interest to citizens' groups, policy makers, graduate students, and other scholars who are interested in doing community studies of this kind.

As a matter of stylistic preference, I have chosen not to interrupt the historical narrative by interjecting personal asides about the research process in the text. There is a natural tendency for the contemporary historian to become drawn into the action as a subject in the drama that he or she is simultaneously observing, analyzing, and reporting from a position that is supposedly at a remove. When that happens, the writer should report her role in the unfolding drama along with everyone else's. But, while my presence was in some ways disturbing, it was not a catalytic presence in either of the two towns, for reasons that I will explain shortly. This is not to say that my work has not had an impact in Somerset County. The impact was to come later, when my dissertation became available to the public.

I did not go into these communities with the object of changing them. My goal was rather to uncover the social, economic, and political structures that have shaped local economic development policy and, at the same time, mediated against democratic social change. Making structures visible is empowering. It allows community members to view their own local history as a work still in progress and to identify the historical junctures where there are real opportunities for them to affect change. I am hopeful, therefore, that this work might provide some encouragement for residents of these and other communities to act for themselves in shaping their own social and economic destinies.

I used the traditional historical method, relying upon published and unpublished historical works, public documents of different kinds, and three newspapers for evidence.[1] I witnessed and recorded contemporary history through direct observation of town meetings, special hearings, meetings of the chambers of commerce, the NAACP, and numerous other public and private forums that I attended and, when possible, taped. These were my primary sources of data. The facts that I report are largely a matter of record.

The particular set of facts that one selects to report depends upon what one considers important. Once selected, the facts still do not speak for themselves; they require analysis and interpretation to give them coherence and meaning. Therefore, to gain background and insight into the way of life in Princess Anne and Crisfield, I composed a list of fifty individuals whom I wanted to interview. I included people whom I identified as important by virtue of the positions they occupied in the civic life of their community, those who had been involved in decisions and events relating to economic development, and key members of groups with a particular stake or interest in the local economy.

Additionally, I included spokespersons for groups that had little means of influencing public policy, in hopes they would inform me about their policy preferences, the factors that influenced their preferences, and what the obstacles to their participation have been. I tried to achieve a balance in terms of race, class, and gender, so that my informants would be reasonably representative of the populations of the two towns along these dimensions.

No sooner had I begun this phase of the research, however, than the plan began to unravel. I quickly learned that many of the people that I thought I needed to talk to had little interest in talking to me. Except in the case of public officeholders and a few marginalized persons and outsiders, my requests for interviews typically went unanswered. My telephone calls were rarely returned.

A small number of people were eager to unburden themselves. They were frustrated by their inability to make their voices heard in their own communities and hoped that I would write something that might attract outside attention to their plight and spur intervention. I did not take everything that was proffered at face value. Realizing that informants' constructions of reality are naturally colored by their interests and values, I weighed the information that they gave me in light of the context in which it was offered and compared it for consistency with evidence that I collected from other sources.

In the beginning, whenever someone agreed to talk with me, I was elated. I went to great lengths to accommodate them, sometimes driving sixty-five miles each way from my home in Delaware for a single appointment. As often as not, when I arrived at the designated meeting place, the person that I had expected to interview was nowhere to be found. I was stood up more often than I care to remember.

I had a different kind of experience with white male elites. Those who were public officeholders felt obligated to grant me an interview, and they kept their appointments. But perhaps because I was a woman and a "student," some treated me with condescension—a strong word, but let me illustrate. The information that these men tendered often amounted to what I began to think of as "the civics lesson." This was an idealized, sterile description of the community that was promulgated for the consumption of outsiders and school children. "No indeed, we don't have any race problems here," was a theme that I heard more than once, but never from blacks. Elite views about women seemed almost as limited as their views about people of color. One prominent civic leader habitually addressed me as "Good Lookin'." When I thanked another man for his time, at the end of an interview, he replied, "I'm glad I could help you with your little paper. That's what you get for being a pretty girl." Whether I was supposed to feel offended or flattered, I am uncertain. But, while I sometimes found these exchanges amusing, I knew that I was not being treated as an adult, much less a professional.

I believe that incidents of this kind help explain why it was unlikely that I could have acted as an *agent provocateur* in Somerset County, even if I had wanted to, and why few local women were visible participants in public life. This was a white man's world if ever there was one. In this insular society, with its established hierarchies of race and gender, the "good-ole-boy" element seemed initially to view me as an insignificant and unwelcome intruder who could be patronized and dismissed. I had the sense that most of the African Americans knew better. They had different reasons for shutting me out.

Given my lack of success in obtaining appointments through telephone "cold calling," I changed strategies and began showing up at public events, striking up conversations with people, and trying to get acquainted with them before asking for interviews. This approach was fairly successful with whites, but many blacks reacted to me with fear and avoidance. I learned that one black leader in Princess Anne had spread word that I was a federal agent operating under cover. I can surmise that this is why certain blacks refused eye contact, turned their backs on me, and walked away whenever I tried to approach them.

This state of affairs seemed highly regrettable for reasons that went beyond the difficulties that it created for the research. My own daily experience of being marginalized and rejected as a woman and an outsider increased my sensitivity to the experience of blacks. The historical research that I had completed before beginning the interviews taught me a great deal about that experience and made me anxious to learn what had been happening to the black population there in the recent era. My concern was thus genuine, and to be perceived as the enemy saddened me. It deepened my lifelong disappointment over the historical and contemporary conditions that have created and perpetuated such deep social cleavages and distrust.

There was another difficulty that cropped up in the interviews. My first forays into the field were to Princess Anne, where I went armed with three different theories that I intended to use as ideal types, a la Max Weber.[2] I would see which of these models provided the best fit with the data. The carefully prepared questions that I would put to selected informants were derived from these theories.

It soon became clear, however, that many of the people who were good enough to grant me interviews were nonplussed by some of my questions and unable to provide me with meaningful answers.

At first, I thought that these questions were confusing to people who were unfamiliar with the intellectual abstractions that political scientists employ as tools of the trade, but that hypothesis proved to be an academic conceit. The real problem went deeper. It appeared that my questions and the theories that they were derived from were largely irrelevant to the daily experience of people who lived in this place, or so it seemed then.

Eventually, I decided to hold all theoretical frameworks in abeyance and allow the communities to reveal their unique shapes and dimensions to me. I stopped trying to steer and control my informants. Figuratively speaking, I sat at their feet—I the student, they the teachers—and allowed them to talk about what seemed important to them. My questions tended to be general and open-ended or requests for elaboration on the themes that they introduced. I tried to understand each bit of information they gave me from their point of view and see how the pieces fit into a coherent picture. I assumed that everything that was said and done had meaning, either overt or hidden, no matter how seemingly unimportant or apparently random it was. I viewed every event as a clue and each piece of data that people revealed, whether willingly or in spite of themselves, as a partial expression of a coherent, underlying reality. The great challenge was to see where those fragments fit into the mosaic that, like an archeologist, I was excavating. I was uncovering an embedded structure.

There were times, too, when I felt as if I were laboring over a giant jigsaw puzzle with no picture on top of the box to refer to. Needless to say, it was frustrating and very slow going. After several weeks of the kinds of experiences described here, I was tired of being condescended to, rejected, brushed off, stood up, and given the run around. I grew concerned that the entire undertaking might have been misconceived and was, therefore, unworkable. With little discernible progress being made on the puzzle, I began to wonder if I should abandon the cause.

But that judgement would have been premature. I have since learned what some of the world's greatest educators have known all along: that the anxiety and confusion that I experienced, first in Princess Anne and later in Crisfield, are an inevitable part of the process of acquiring genuine new knowledge.[3] How can it be otherwise when we relinquish the security of our well-worn paradigms and, no longer relying upon the received wisdom, venture into unfamiliar terrain?

In my case, there came a time when I did not know if I could go on with the work. Not only did my intellectual confusion persist, but I felt intimidated by some of the people in Princess Anne. I had found the town manager's demeanor decidedly menacing. I experienced the fear that I sensed in many nonelites, especially blacks. While *fear* might seem to be an exaggerated reaction in this context, I trust that as the history of Somerset County unfolds in the following pages, the aptness of that emotion will become more apparent. People who have a dream of social and political transformation live with fear. In the words of a famous Brazilian scholar, "If your dream was to preserve the status quo, what should you fear then? . . . [but] if your dream is transformation, then you fear the reaction of the powers that are now in power."[4] I believe that that is why many blacks were afraid.

As for me, I came into Somerset County probing the social, economic, and political structures that, for three hundred years, had militated against democratic social change. My research agenda was therefore highly political. While I have truly stated that I did not go into these communities as an agent of change, it is nonetheless also true that, in the county's repressive political culture, merely to ask certain questions was construed by ruling elites as a challenge. It was unavoidable that, in attempting to deconstruct the prevailing myths or "civics lessons," I would call into question those constructions of reality that served to justify and perpetuate the prevailing regime. In so doing, I provoked reaction and risk. It was therefore entirely predictable that I and the people who were willing to talk with me would sometimes feel afraid. But when my morale was about at its lowest ebb, the words of a familiar song began coming into my mind as a constant refrain.

> Keep your hand on that plough.
> Hold on! Why don't you hold on?
> Keep your eyes on the prize.
> Hold on! Why don't you hold on?

What better advice could there be for anyone struggling alone in the field?

At last, there came a turning point, when I gained the trust of key individuals, and they introduced me to others who talked with me frankly. Discretion forbids me to identify those persons, but I am lastingly grateful to them, and they know who they are. As a stranger, I was given the brush-off or trite civics lessons by people who were either afraid of me or had something to hide. I was deeply touched by others who, without knowing me, took me into their confidence and staked their own security and reputations upon my trustworthiness. Thanks to them, I began to hit pay dirt.

The same thing happened in Crisfield the following year. After a slow start, I found individuals who not only gave me candid interviews but also provided me with entrees to their relatives, friends, and associates. For example, I was introduced to key members of Crisfield's black community as the result of this moving encounter. One afternoon in midsummer, I was interviewing an African American matron who, because of her many spiritual gifts and good works, was known in the black community as a great holy woman. I was comfortable in her presence and sensed a rapport between us. Then, midway through our conversation, her eyes filled with tears as she said, "The Holy Spirit testifies to my spirit that God sent you here to help us, the poor and downtrodden in this community, both blacks and whites. He tells me to tell you not to be afraid or discouraged, but to keep on with your work until it is finished. He tells me I'm to help you and lead you to others who can help you more than I can." She later introduced me to other African Americans whose assistance advanced the work greatly.

When I brought my research to a close in 1991, I had interviewed forty-eight people, some repeatedly. Of this number, ten were blacks—mostly respected leaders in Princess Anne and Crisfield. I am sad to report that, in the end, I had interviewed only seven women, and all but one of them were middle-class whites. This is because men so dominated public life and local politics that it was unusual for women to participate in or even demonstrate an informed awareness about civic life outside the domains traditionally reserved for them. Those domains include voluntary and paid work in libraries, hospitals, schools, and churches, and participation in beauty contests and other festivals, but not community political and economic development. Opportunities for women of color were even more limited.

I confess to a sense of puzzlement over the criticism of some readers that this study fails to talk about poor whites. I do not know what these readers could have been looking for. Did they have in mind a certain stereotype—dirt farmers tilling "God's little acre" or perhaps people not working at all? Apparently they were not anticipating the watermen—people of dignity and independence, though many were not well off and few had a high level of education. They participated in a subsistence economy but led rich lives anyway, which is something that most academics might not expect. In fact, the term *poor whites* does not appear in this study, because, as a southerner, I find it demeaning. It is too suggestive of the expression "poor white trash." Therefore, when writing about poor elements of the white population, I have chosen to use other expressions, such as the *watermen*, which do not, I hope, diminish the dignity of the people I am writing about.

The perspective that I developed in the course of the fieldwork grew out of the fact that I went into Somerset County as a powerless person and an outsider, and I was received by other powerless people and outsiders who were willing to share their perspective with me. They were unpracticed in exclusionary politics, for they had not run the county and had nothing to hide. Moreover, their values were consistent with those of the larger public: values of democracy, equality, the right to dissent. There were other perspectives on these communities, to be sure, but I was not made privy to them. The county's ruling elites did not confide in me, for they were unaccustomed to opening up for scrutiny their conduct of public affairs.

It may be especially remarkable that the mayor of Crisfield was open despite being an officeholder. I attribute this to the fact that he held power in the formal sense, but not as a participant in an insiders' game. Mayor Scott's exercise of power was open and public. While he was not a person with a high level of education, he was nevertheless able to accept my inquiry at face value. In this sense, he was atypical, for key powerholders were accustomed to withholding disclosure as a way of avoiding accountability. Their actions nevertheless had consequences for others in the community, and I have reported the perspective of these "others" in their own words whenever it seemed safe to do so.

I used a tape recorder, at first, in my interviews, but I abandoned the practice, because it unnerved people. I offered my pledge of confidentiality to all my informants, realizing that this was the only condition under which most people would talk with me frankly. I also deemed it necessary for their protection, and I still do. A few public figures declined this offer, saying that they preferred to speak openly and for the record. Those individuals are quoted by name; the rest required anonymity.

My inauspicious beginnings in Princess Anne and Crisfield did not prevent me from acquiring a profound admiration for certain individuals whom I got to know and had occasion to observe in the performance of their civic roles over a period of years. They were black and white, male and female, rich and poor, and they varied greatly in social class and educational attainment. Still, each appeared to identify with his or her community as a whole, including all of its members, even though some of them were stigmatized by that same community because of their race, class, gender, lifestyle, or status as outsiders.

What these special citizens all had in common was that they were engaged in efforts to build or maintain genuinely democratic institutions and culture in communities where democratic traditions were fragile or had not taken root. I also found them to be among the most interesting people that I have met, because, far from engaging in a perpetual calculation of self-interest, they frequently reflected upon larger questions of rights and liberties, justice, equality, and the meaning of democracy and the general good in the specific context of life in their own small communities. What is more, they gave concrete expression to their moral insights through their public actions. Their universalistic worldview seemed actually to enlarge their humanity. Perhaps it is not accidental that citizens of this calibre are to be found in American political communities that are no larger than ancient Greek city-states, for their distinguishing attribute, to my mind, is their civic virtue.[6]

I have reported that it became necessary for me to hold my theoretical frameworks in suspension, because they interfered with my ability to discover and account for anomalies, of which there were many in Somerset County. However, there came a time in each community when someone supplied me with an insight or bit of new information that, by its essential *pars-pro-toto* function, suddenly allowed me to see how the theories that I had put aside could be brought together in a new synthesis.[7] When this happened, it was like a *Gestalt*. By expanding the regime framework to incorporate key tenets of the growth-machine thesis and the culturalist school, I was able to transcend the traditional urban-rural duality, which was the cause of my earlier theoretical impasse, and bring the outlines of an embedded structure into view. After that, filling in the remaining pieces was almost mechanical.

Next came the task of verifying my conclusions. This was a straightforward process of empirical validation through more interviews and references to the historical and documentary record. While informant interviews were essential to gain understanding, it is important to emphasize that this book is based solidly in historical facts. Specifically, the 1990 elections in Princess Anne (chapter 4) and Crisfield's experience with Project Phoenix (chapter 5) present closely documented, empirical evidence in support of my thesis. To say this, however, is not to diminish the importance of interviews.[8] It is, after all, gruesome to contemplate how devoid of truth, life, and meaning are facts that are presented without understanding.

ACKNOWLEDGMENTS

The gratitude that I feel as I write these acknowledgments is tinged with sadness, because one to whom I owe a very great intellectual and spiritual debt is no longer among us—Professor Norton E. Long. He inspired, encouraged, and assisted me in this undertaking. I have lost a great friend.

To Clarence N. Stone, who directed the dissertation upon which this work is based, I owe an incalculable intellectual debt. I am no less grateful to him for the confidence he expressed, on many occasions, that this work would not only be published but would be widely read. Anyone who has ever been a graduate student knows how much those words mean! Todd Swanstrom offered scholarly criticism and suggestions that helped make this prophecy a reality and provided indispensable moral support every step of the way. I am deeply indebted to him too.

Many people read parts of the manuscript at different stages of its evolution and offered important suggestions. Among them are George Callcott, Alexander Bourgeois, John A. Bourgeois, Denis Goulet, Morris Lounds, Harvey Molotch, Daniel Monti, Edward Smith Ramsay, John R. Wennersten, and Warren Van Wycklin.

Ryan Nelson of Washington, D.C., donated the drawing in chapter 4. Credit for the photography goes to Claude Wiles of Princess Anne, Maryland. I owe special thanks to David Bremer of the *Crisfield Times* and Richard Crumbacker of the *Somerset Herald*, because these two newspaper editors cooperated generously and extensively with the documentary research. I wish that it were possible for me openly to acknowledge others who offered important assistance, but they preferred to make their contributions anonymously.

I am grateful to Clay Morgan, Acquisitions Editor; Elizabeth Moore, Production Editor; and David J. Vogler, the editor in whose series this book appears. Their professional assistance and steady encouragement made the State University of New York Press a pleasure to work with. I am also indebted to several anonymous reviewers for their fine suggestions on how to improve the final product presented here.

I am proud to acknowledge Kurt Finsterbusch, my husband, teacher, and friend. He bolstered my spirits when the going was rough and offered unflagging good counsel. Just as important were the many scholarly insights and suggestions that he gave me and that I incorporated throughout this work.

Finally, I am most deeply indebted to the good citizens of Somerset County who offered their hospitality to a stranger. Without their generous assistance, this work would not have been possible. My book is dedicated to them.

1

INTRODUCTION

Princess Anne and Crisfield, Maryland, are both located in Somerset County, where the official motto is *Semper Eadem*—ever the same. And it is indeed surprising how little has changed there in the more than three hundred years that have passed since its founding.[1] When it was established in 1666, Somerset was the poorest county on Maryland's Eastern Shore. On the eve of the Civil War, it was one of the poorest in the state. The county spent virtually nothing for schools or for road maintenance then, nor did it make any public expenditures for the poor.[2] After the Civil War, an economic renaissance occurred that was stimulated by the coming of the railroad, new farming technologies, and an oystering boom that reached its peak in the 1880s and continued for several decades thereafter. The prosperity during that period was extraordinary; unfortunately, it did not last. Throughout most of the twentieth century, Somerset has experienced population loss and economic decline.

The Great Depression marked the beginning of a long and still continuing outmigration. By 1910, the county's population had peaked at 26,455, where it remained fairly stable until the 1930s. During that decade, numerous farms and businesses were lost.[3]

Between 1940 and 1980, while the rest of Maryland experienced the fastest population growth in its history, Somerset County alone declined in population.[4] In 1990, it had about 21,000 residents, with 1,666 living in Princess Anne and 2,880 in Crisfield.[5] By 1986, Somerset had fallen behind even the poorest Appalachian counties in western Maryland and thus became the poorest county in the state. There was no movie theatre, no department store, no public transportation. The average income was less than eight thousand dollars.

FIGURE 1.1 Semper Eadem: Change Comes Slowly in the
Somerset County Courthouse

When I first ventured into Somerset County as a research assistant investigating the outcome of job generating activities there, I naturally assumed that in this poorest of all Maryland counties, the residents would overwhelmingly favor growth.[6] Moreover, because the study of small town and rural regimes had remained theoretically and empirically underdeveloped,[7] the ideology of growth boosterism that was continuously promulgated by economic development officials and chambers of commerce had become the conventional wisdom by default, even among scholars. Derived from nineteenth-century neoclassical economic theory, the dominant view in the 1980s was that growth is conducive to a community's overall good. Promoting growth through top-down economic development strategies is politically popular too, because residents can see that their individual interests are tied to the level of commercial activity in their town.[8] Elected officials were thus expected to pursue development for the sake of the public interest and to enhance their political standing as well. Persuaded by the simple, deductive logic of the market model, I too expected that the greater a community's economic distress, the greater the popular sentiment in favor of development activities would be.[9] And indeed, survey data indicate that most Somerset County residents favor economic growth.[10]

FIGURE 1.2 This Store on Smith Island Is a Popular Gathering Place

Readers might therefore share my surprise that my interviews with individuals in Princess Anne and Crisfield revealed a deep, pervasive ambivalence about economic development. What was going on? Even more baffling was the fact that, while both towns were experiencing similar levels of economic distress, their development policies differed markedly from each other.

The theoretical impasse that I encountered in the course of that first research project was, in fact, entirely predictable, for Martin Staniland has shown that there is an intractable logical problem inherent in any explanation of development policy that is based upon general economic models.[11] The problem can be briefly stated as follows: If one assumes that people in different communities are more or less equally rational, then what can account for the variety of policy responses in communities experiencing similar levels of economic distress? The market model, by itself, is inadequate to explain this variation, because, although it tells us that individuals seek to maximize their utility, it fails to explain how individuals acquire one set of preferences instead of another.

There is a promising alternative to the market model, however, that is sometimes referred to as the "social embeddedness argument." As Mark Granovetter explains it, "Actors do not behave or decide as atoms outside a social context, nor do they adhere slavishly to a script written for them by the particular intersection of social categories that they happen to occupy. Their attempts at purposive action are instead imbedded in concrete, ongoing systems of social relations."[12] My general aim in pursuing this research was to examine Somerset's two towns, which were experiencing similar levels of economic distress, and explain their different development policies in terms of the social embeddedness argument advanced by Granovetter and other scholars.[13]

I accept individual rationality as given. I assume that people are capable of being purposeful, deliberative, and prudent in their choices among the alternative courses of action available to them. The task, then, was not to determine whether decisionmakers in Princess Anne and Crisfield acted to maximize their individual interest, or the interest of their community as a whole, but rather to learn how historical events and the unique way of life in these places might have mediated policy responses to economic pressures by shaping the values of individuals and thus their perceptions of what their interests were.

But explaining preference formation cannot, by itself, provide a full understanding of economic development policy, because, even within a single community, policy preferences vary. Princess Anne and Crisfield both lacked a unifying vision of how best to respond to economic decline. A complete explanation of their different policies therefore also requires an analysis of the political processes by which some preferences were selected instead of others. Hence the research task was two-fold: It involved an analysis of how local history, social structures, and culture molded the policy preferences of individuals, and it also required an explanation of how these variables shaped policy decisions about economic development in the two towns.

I understand social structures to be sets of incentives and constraints that regulate behavior and are embodied in the patterned actions of individuals.[14] A regime is such a structure, and the institution of slavery is another example. By defining opportunities and limits that guide, restrain, and inspire individual action, they inculcate a shared worldview that includes meanings, values, and expectations.

Social structures that are rooted in particular places tend to generate local culture. Because social structures exist in a dynamic and reciprocal relationship with the mindsets or cultures that they engender, this study treats culture and structure together, viewing them as closely-linked processes that continuously shape and perpetuate a community's way of life. It also assumes that social structures can be explained in terms of an interaction between the desirability of their consequences for different groups and the relative power of those groups.[15] An analysis of local power relations was therefore essential to this inquiry, and urban regime theory provided the theoretical framework.

Chapter 2 presents the relevant theories in greater detail and explains the historical method that guided this research. Because the major theoretical position involves local regimes, it was necessary that the research be expansive enough to include the formation and maintenance of those regimes as well as decision processes directly related to development policy. While one may view the policy outputs of local governments as the product of economic, social, and political processes that characterize the prevailing regime, a particular regime may itself be viewed as the product of economic, social, and political processes occurring through time. A regime must be understood, then, as both cause and consequence of ongoing historical processes.[16] Abrams explains this "two-sidedness" of the social world as "the ways in which, in time, actions become institutions and institutions are in turn changed by actions."[17] The crucial point is that the link between social structures and social action is the historical process.

Chapter 3 presents a three-hundred-year history of Somerset County's adaptations to potentially restructuring events—that is, internal and external events that might have brought about a fundamental restructuring of the social order.[18] When I first conceived this portion of the research, I intended for the broad historical chapter to serve as mere prologue to the heart of the research project— the twin case studies of Princess Anne and Crisfield. But now I judge it to be on a par with these chapters and perhaps even the centerpiece. It returns to the first inhabitants of the county and the entire Chesapeake region and shows how their economic, political, and social history is related to the prevailing way of life in Princess Anne and Crisfield in the recent era, still shaping political and economic decisions and outcomes for the future. It reveals who was most invested in and who was least attached to these historical institutions and reports the buildup of pressures that threatened to undermine their foundations. The almost unvarying pattern of resistance to change that unfolds over a three-hundred-year period is itself as powerful a testimony to the central thesis of this book as anything that follows it.

But the social structure of Somerset County was complex, and there were opposing tendencies in its two sectors. Chapters 4 and 5 present case studies of Princess Anne and Crisfield during the five years between 1986 and 1991, when both communities were in the throes of serious economic decline and active efforts to respond were taking shape. They demonstrate in close detail how the way of life in the two towns varied and how this led to a marked variance in their responses to economic pressures. Chapter 4 relates how Princess Anne, the commercial center for the county's agricultural industry, first succumbed to a land-based growth machine and then overthrew it, only to have it re-establish its control of the town government within six months. Chapter 5 details how Crisfield controlled growth in order to protect its fragile seafood industry, the traditional way of life that was based upon it, and the subsistence requirements of the poor population. It thus adds a new category to existing American political typologies by describing what I have called a "subsistence regime."

Chapter 6 presents the analysis and the conclusion. By explaining why two towns in the same county responded in such different ways to economic decline, this work empirically demonstrates a theoretical principle of broad significance. Because specific types of economies support certain ways of life and not others, major economic change threatens to upset established power relations, degrade cultural values, and disrupt fragile subsistence arrangements, to mention only a few of its sociocultural impacts. Goulet says that "development is necessary, because all societies must come to terms with new aspirations and irresistible social forces," and there are few students of American government who would disagree with this statement.[19] "Yet the choices they face are cruel," he continues, "because development's benefits are obtained only at a great price, and because, on balance, it is far from certain that development's benefits make men happier or freer."[20] It is this second statement that commands our attention, because it jolts whatever complacent assumptions one might harbor that economic development's impacts are always, or for the most part, benign.

Economic development acts like a giant asphalt paving machine that tears up the old road in the process of building the new.[21] Contrary to some ideologies of the political Left, it is not the bourgeoisie alone that benefits from existing economic arrangements (although one might argue that it profits the most). These case studies demonstrate that different elements in Somerset County were attached to different aspects of the traditional way of life there, and individuals from virtually all walks of life worried about potential impacts of development projects that threatened to introduce far reaching social change. All were participants in a shared way of life that they continued to cling to.

Contrary to some ideologies of the political Right that view values as deriving from economic interests, these case studies show that the marketplace justifications that were offered for proposed development projects did not represent the operative value systems of many of the people who would directly experience their impacts. This explains why, despite survey data that indicate widespread local support for the idea of economic growth, top down development projects encountered sustained opposition. Typically, they were conceived in secret and implementation was attempted with little regard for their impacts on the social structure or the nonmaterial values of local residents. Just as important, individuals construed even their economic interests within a context of ongoing social and economic arrangements, therefore, projects that were promoted as "developmental" but threatened to upset these arrangements were viewed by various groups as potentially harmful to their economic interests too.

To recognize that there was a nearly universal commitment to a shared way of life in Somerset County is not to minimize the importance of ideological divisions and deep racial and social-class tensions that characterized this community. Some elements in the county felt that existing arrangements afforded them precious few benefits and thoroughgoing economic development would be advantageous for them individually and for their community. Some members of the black community were of this opinion, and so were some governing elites and working-class whites. But whether or not their policy preferences prevailed largely depended upon their place in the social order.

In Princess Anne, for example, where the traditional "court-house elites" could no longer sustain themselves in a declining agri-cultural economy and thus became willing to accept economic change, development was placed high on the agenda. But when pol-icy preferences of subordinate groups conflicted with those of more powerful elements in the towns and county, their concerns tended not to be given a hearing. For this reason, and because these cases demonstrate that preferences are not autonomous or "given," but are instead shaped by the unique set of opportunities and con-straints that individuals encounter in the concrete circumstances of their lives, it is clear that the structural and cultural features of a particular community can be more powerful mediators of economic development policy than many sociologists, political scientists and economists have supposed. The considerable policy implications of this are discussed in the last chapter.

One might object, of course, that Princess Anne and Crisfield are small Gemeinschaft communities and their experience may dif-fer from that of large cities. Without question, there are important differences between human settlements of different sizes, and to argue otherwise would be foolish. But the urban-rural dichotomy that views traditional social relations as the exclusive preserve of small towns and rural communities is seriously misleading, and to continue to cling to it is to ignore a vast reservoir of empirical evi-dence to the contrary. This point will be taken up again in the next chapter.

Finally, local communities and the regimes that arise out of them powerfully shape economic opportunities and constraints for different groups according to the place of those groups in the social order. Therefore, community and state should not be viewed as existing apart from or in opposition to the market, for they are integral to it. Whether in rural areas in the Third World, the new "global cities," or small towns on the Eastern Shore, all economies are enmeshed in the political, social, and moral life of particular places. Based on this understanding, the chapters that follow present an empirical argument that economic change can have far-reaching political and sociocultural impacts. Therefore, economic decline and development alike should be viewed as instigating events. And because the policy responses of local regimes are also embedded in historically given systems of social relations, the values that regimes seek to advance and protect by the economic policies they pursue may include, but are not necessarily dominated by, profit motives. Indeed, the case studies presented here show that economic development stances and individual action were frequently prompted by other, less instrumental values that superceded egoistic profit maximization, because, among other things, community mattered.

2

Theoretical Frameworks

A wealth of research chronicles the struggle of American cities, small towns, and rural communities to maintain their fiscal viability in the wake of the global restructuring of markets that has been occurring since World War II. Scholars note that localities compete with other localities to attract industry, jobs, and capital investment,[1] and this observation raises important questions for the social sciences. One of the most influential theories in the economic development literature posits that behavior is market driven and interprets the policy choices of local governments as rational responses to economic imperatives. For example, Paul Peterson has viewed cities operating like corporations in competition with other cities to attract mobile capital. In his book *City Limits*, he argues that this policy not only maximizes profits for local businesses, but, more important, it is essential to the unitary good of the whole community.[2]

But critics of the market model have rejected its economic determinism and challenged its Utopian assumption that the material well-being of business elites is generally coterminous with some identifiable good of the whole community.[3] Market forces, far from resulting in an overarching public good, often inflict social and material harms on some groups while conferring inordinate benefits on others. Therefore, economic rationality, by itself, cannot adequately explain development policy. Clearly, the exercise of political power must be involved.

Polanyi was among the first to challenge the neoclassical economic theory on which the market model is based. By demonstrating historically that unregulated market forces are destructive to society itself and thus inevitably arouse resistance and stir up countermovements, he showed that markets, far from ever being "free," are of necessity created and sustained by public authority.[4] There are three principles here, and each deserves emphasis. First, Polanyi exposes the functionalist fallacy in classical and neoclassical economic theory by showing that market forces harm society. Second, he shows that, because of the widespread social harms they inflict, unregulated market forces inevitably generate conflict. And third, he insists upon the fundamental role of the state, not only in creating markets in the first place but also in maintaining them through the regulation and containment of their deleterious social effects. Polanyi's brilliant exposition of the role of political power and public authority in creating and maintaining the so-called free market economy demonstrates the need for a structural approach to the analysis of economic development policy. In other words, he shows why politics matters.

More recent scholars have deepened the critique of the market model by attacking its utilitarian underpinnings. Martin Staniland, discussing the variety of responses to market forces in peasant societies, addresses the problem as follows:

> Calculations of individual interest are not made in isolation, and rationality itself is contingent on a selection of values and preferences . . . why do peasants have some preferences rather than others, and how is their range of values shaped in the first place? Such questions require an explanatory framework that is 'social' or 'cultural' in scope. To say that individuals 'pursue their interests' or 'maximize their utility' sounds toughmindedly realistic, but only until we start asking why 'reality' is seen differently by people who are presumably equally rational.[5]

Addressing the same problem, Mark Granovetter also advanced the view that the preferences of individuals are not autonomous or "given" but are instead formed within particular social contexts. This has come to be known as the "social embeddedness argument."[6] An earlier, related theme that concerns the importance of local political arrangements was developed in the community power literature, beginning in the 1950s with Floyd Hunter's *Community Power Structure.*[7] Hunter's work inspired a host of other important community studies, such as Robert Dahl's classic *Who Governs?*[8] But this once fruitful avenue of inquiry became diverted into a sterile debate between proponents of the elitist and the pluralist schools and eventually faded out.[9]

URBAN REGIME THEORY

Urban regime theory is a development in urban scholarship that began in the 1980s and has strong intellectual roots in the community power tradition.[10] By adopting a political economy approach, it moves the study of urban politics beyond the pluralist-elitist debate.[11] This new paradigm offers a broad explanatory framework that assigns central importance to the informal processes of collaboration between those who control investment capital (and other privately held resources) and those who control government authority. Given the "division of labor between state and market" in a capitalist democracy,[12] such collaboration is viewed as necessary for the achievement of major public initiatives at the local level. Clarence Stone's analysis of how governing capacity is enlarged by the parceling out of small opportunities and selective incentives in order to sustain governing coalitions underscores with fresh force and precision the extent to which politics matters.[13]

But with the exception of Richard DeLeon's book *Left Coast City* that focuses on the centrality of civic culture in the progressive politics in San Francisco, little weight has been given to cultural variables by scholars who work with regime theory.[14] Todd Swanstrom charges that "American political scientists have always been fearful of the effects of the passions of race, ethnicity, nationalism, or moral fervor and more comfortable with 'interests.'"[15] Invoking the social embeddedness argument, he urges scholars to direct close attention to the cultural context in which economic restructuring occurs, for in this respect, urban regime theory remains underdeveloped.

The present work embraces this intellectual challenge. It goes beyond existing regime analyses in the extent to which it focuses on the particular way of life in local communities. Its close study of the life-patterning social structures and culture that shape decision making with regard to economic development in two towns further elaborates this important new paradigm.

THE MARKET MODEL

Peterson intends for his market model to serve as a critique of established theories for what he sees as their excessive reliance on political variables and their inadequate recognition of the economic factors that constrain public policy in American cities. To correct this imbalance, he likens the city to a business firm. Just as the firm has a corporate interest apart from the interests and preferences of its employees, the city has a unitary interest apart from the interests and preferences of its individual residents. While individual and group preferences within a city may be diverse and conflictual, there is nevertheless a common understanding as to what constitutes the interest of the city per se. Just as business firms must compete with other business firms for customers and profits, the unitary interest of cities requires that they compete with other cities to attract and retain mobile capital.

Economically dependent upon private investment, cities are driven to pursue a policy of courting outside industry by creating a "favorable business climate" that is conducive to capital accumulation and economic growth. This often translates into tax abatements and low-interest, long-term loans for businesses. Costly upgrading of municipal infrastructures and other subsidies may also be granted to attract, accommodate, and retain business investment.

Peterson's special insight is that cities are limited in the policies they can pursue, because it is only private investment that can provide the jobs and tax base that are the indirect source of public spending capacity for local governments in the United States. Cities are limited by their lack of legal authority to impose tariffs, regulate commerce, or control in and out migration across their borders. The difference between cities and the national government in this regard is a function of the structural relationship between the different levels of government in the federal system. The result of these structural limitations is that localities are forced to compete with other localities, and increasingly with Third World nations, to attract employment and business investments that will sustain or elevate the local tax base.

Cities act always to advance their interest in economic efficiency, according to Peterson, which "all but precludes a concern for redistribution."[16] The redistributive function that local governments are unable, in his view, to perform must be taken up by the national government. However, City Limits was published in 1981 before the impacts of Ronald Reagan's "new federalism" became clear. In fact, budgetary constraints upon the national government in recent years have lent force to a conservative movement for retrenchment in federal redistributive policies and devolution of responsibility for social programs to the states. Reagan's new federalism, in effect now for more than a decade, has drastically reduced the role of the federal government in a wide range of programs and services for the disadvantaged and greatly increased the redistributional burden on state and local governments.

Peterson concedes that there is conflict over local policies, given the diversity of individual and group preferences and the fact that "factions and groups may put their separate interests ahead of that of the community."[17] The self-interested factions to which he refers are most likely to be workers, minorities, the unemployed, and the poor, because "it is the interests of the disadvantaged that consistently come into conflict with economically productive policies," which he equates with the unitary interest of the community.[18] Conflict is low, however, because the participation of disadvantaged groups historically has been limited, and access also remains largely restricted to political and economic elites. Even so, a residual amount of conflict will remain. But given the structural features that so sharply limit the policy choices for cities, "the political variables no longer remain relevant to the analysis."[19]

The central hypothesis of the market model can be stated as follows: Cities are rational entities that maximize their economic return, and this translates into a policy of pursuing capital investment for the benefit the entire community, while eschewing redistributive social programs because they benefit only a part of the community to the detriment of the whole. Then Peterson considers it only a minor simplification to state that "cities are above all concerned with their economic well-being."[20] He acknowledges that exceptions may be found in certain suburban areas and small cities where status objectives predominate over economic interests, or where consensus may break down into conflict between those who favor promoting economic growth and those who wish to survive as an exclusive residential enclave. These exceptions pertain, however, where proximity to major markets provides the economic base to sustain prosperity in an exclusively residential community.[21]

Given the eroding tax base of rural counties throughout the 1980s and the well-documented pattern of concern among those counties to attract new business investment and create more jobs, it is entirely plausible that municipalities in a county that is economically distressed and remote from major markets might conform to the market model.[22] Such was not the case, however, either in Princess Anne or in Crisfield during the period covered by this research. The regime analyses presented in chapters 3, 4, and 5 will show that while both communities were experiencing serious economic decline, issues of security, identity, status, and role in a given social order and commitment to a particular set of values and way of life prevailed over economic maximization to determine policy stances at times and also acted as barriers to development. Politics, whether rural or urban, is not the expression of material interests alone, but also of "passions rooted in place, deeply felt identities of race and ethnicity, thoughtful commitments to a sense of justice and fairness."[23] For these and other reasons, the market model is inadequate, by itself, to explain economic development policy in Princess Anne and Crisfield.

THE GROWTH MACHINE THESIS

An important contribution to the urban political economy literature is Logan and Molotch's widely cited *Urban Fortunes*.[24] These scholars stress the informal, collusive aspects of local governance. "An apparatus of interlocking pro-growth associations and governmental units" makes up the coalition that Molotch, in an earlier article, called the "growth machine."[25]

Logan and Molotch view land-based elites as colluding with each other and government officials to achieve land-use intensification and thus enhanced rents for personal gain. People who are drawn into local politics tend to be businessmen whose motives, at least initially, are to "wheel and deal" to affect land-use and resource distribution, which is the essence of local politics, in this view. Those who participate in local affairs, particularly local government, and those to whom they are most responsive once in office, are the people who have the most to gain or lose in decisions affecting land use. The local newspaper, whose levels of profitability are tied to the aggregate growth or decline in the locality, is often prominent in the coalition: "The newspaper has no ax to grind except the one that holds the community elite together: growth."[26] Utilities, real estate interests, lawyers, chambers of commerce, and local financial institutions also play on this team. Together they generate "the community 'we feeling' (or perhaps more aptly the 'our feeling') that comes to be an influence in the politics of a given locality."[27] Growth is the closest thing there is to a "common interest," in Molotch's view, although many city residents are harmed by it, and inordinate benefits are garnered by a limited few. "The city is, for those who count, a growth machine."[28]

Those who do not "count" tend to be people who view the city as their home. The 'use values' and 'exchange values' of land are concepts that Logan and Molotch have elaborated in *Urban Fortunes*.[29] Use values are the characteristics and amenities of a place that matter to people who live there. Exchange values determine its worth in the market for the "place entrepreneurs," or "modern rentiers," as Logan and Molotch have called the growth interests.

These authors see an inherent contradiction between use and exchange values of place, because, as the city is increasingly transformed into a bundle of commodities by the growth machine, other values and concerns are correspondingly displaced. For this reason, "additional local growth under current arrangements is a transfer of wealth and life chances from the general public to the rentier groups and their associates. Use values of a majority are sacrificed for the exchange values of a few."[30] An unanswered question is how this happens if elections are viewed as vehicles of popular control, as some democratic theories assume. The growth machine thesis is consistent with urban regime theory in its focus on the informal, coalitional aspect of local governance and its rejection of the naive view that policy is determined by votes.

TOWARD A NEW SYNTHESIS

The political economy approach to urban politics takes popular participation in elections as a factor of given importance and, at the same time, acknowledges that private control of investment decisions is centrally important. A regime is conceived as a set of informal arrangements by which governing bodies and actors in the private sector combine resources in order to augment their capacities. Regime theorists hold that local policy outcomes represent real political choices that are shaped by a confluence of variables affecting the character of regimes and the kinds of growth policies they pursue. According to Stone, these factors include the composition of the ruling group, the terms on which its members are related, and the nature of the resources it controls.[31] Swanstrom further posits that a regime's economic policy will depend upon fiscal pressures, the prevailing mode of capital accumulation, the social structure of the local community, and the normative values upheld by the ruling group.[32] This theory's special utility as a framework for the present research lies in its capacity to illuminate a range of informal social, economic, and political relationships that shape policy responses to economic decline.

Empirical research using urban regime theory has been limited, for the most part, to case studies of large cities. But this book's application of it to non-metropolitan communities demonstrates that, like the growth machine thesis, regime theory can illuminate community power relations and political processes in human settlements of different sizes. The theory required further development, however, in order to encompass the traditional way-of-life variables that intellectual convention has consigned to small towns and rural communities only. In the remainder of this chapter, I will argue that the urban-rural duality is misleading and propose a new theoretical synthesis that fully incorporates traditional social structures and culture into the regime paradigm.

The Urban-Rural Duality

The Gemeinschaft-Gesellschaft duality posed by Toennies has calcified into an intellectual tradition that continues to shape our thinking about social relations in small towns and in large cities. It has become conventional to treat the study of cities and rural communities as antithetical. They are studied as different fields, each with its own professional societies, conferences, and journals. Urbanists tend to disdain rural studies, and ruralists often evince a similar lack of interest in urban scholarship. Because students of local government tend thus to rule out commonalities between settlements of different sizes a priori, and, in so doing, forego important insights and promising avenues of inquiry, it is important to try to bridge this dichotomy.[33] It may be more useful to view these different categories as variants of a single phenomenon—the local community.

Certainly rural communities lack the complexity of metropolitan environments. There are places in the mountain hollows of Appalachia, the bayou country of southwest Louisiana, and on Maryland and Virginia's Eastern Shore where local polities are barely distinct from extended family networks or church congregations. Such communities seem, at first glance, to represent one pole of the urban-rural dichotomy that was given its most comprehensive expression in a classic essay by Louis Wirth.

Wirth argued that Gemeinschaft is the traditional, personal, and communal way of life that is based upon family and kinship ties in small towns and rural communities, while Gesellschaft, or "urbanism," as he called it, is a way of life characterized by rational, instrumental social relations that are "impersonal, superficial, transitory, and segmental," and based upon interest.[34] "The reserve, the indifference, and the blase outlook which urbanites manifest in their relationships may be regarded as devices for immunizing themselves against the personal claims and expectations of others."[35] The underlying causes of urbanism, in Wirth's view, are the size, density, and heterogeneity of urban populations.

My own position is that the urban-rural duality is misleading. With Bender, I would argue that it is fundamentally ahistorical, for it implies a sense of the past that is made up of ideal types linked only by logical necessity, and "this logic fails to oblige the theorist to analyze structural change as a temporally and culturally situated process."[36] Theories that incorporate these ideal types (e.g., modernization theory), "lack a firm attachment to the historical record of social change over the course of American history and as a result, offer a logic of history rather than a historically grounded account of social change."[37] Furthermore, they impede our ability to recognize structural and cultural continuities in communities of different sizes.

Reviewing the empirical evidence that has built up over the decades, Bender cites Lewis's 1952 case study of urbanization in Mexico City, Morse's 1959 study of Latin American cities, and Foley's 1952 study of Rochester, New York, all of which show that urbanization did not transform social relations in the way that Wirth's essay predicts. He also cites surveys by Bell, Greer, Janowitz, and others, which revealed that "social relationships that might be communal remained important, even in the largest cities."[38] Bender additionally cites Litwack, Sussman, Gans, Suttles, Feagin, Stack, and Freid, who "showed that ethnic, class, and racial neighborhoods persisted in the city and that primary relationships provided the social foundation for them."[39] Collectively, these works offer a formidable body of evidence that is contrary to the urban-rural duality.

Summarizing his argument that rationality and traditionalism, Gemeinschaft and Gesellschaft, are modes of action that are inherent to all social life, Bender concludes that in some cases urbanization can actually increase ethnic identification and what sociologists call 'primordial ties.' . . . The task is not to date the moment when one of the worlds of social relations is replaced by the other; it is to probe their interaction and to assess their relative salience to people's lives in specific situations."[40]

Gans joins Bender in challenging the urban-rural duality. He offers three objections to Wirth's formulation.

First, the conclusions derived from a study of the inner city cannot be generalized to the entire urban area. Second, there is as yet not enough evidence to prove—or, admittedly, to deny— that number, density, and heterogeneity result in the social consequences which Wirth proposed. Finally, even if the causal relationship could be verified, it can be shown that a significant proportion of the city's inhabitants were, and are, isolated from these consequences by social structures and cultural patterns which they either brought to the city or developed by living in it.[41]

Claude Fischer's subcultural theory of urbanism would seem to support the Wirthian duality, at least partially, by arguing that urban living provides individuals with alternatives to reliance upon relatives and thus results in reduced interaction with kin. But recent research instead supports Gans's view that urbanism, by itself, has no independent effect upon social relationships. Thomas C. Wilson has analyzed national survey data in order to test Wirth's claim that urbanism weakens kinship bonds and reduces the social significance of the family. He finds that urban families are just as close-knit and just as likely to rely upon one another as those elsewhere. Wilson concludes: "It seems very doubtful that a general weakening of kinship bonds is an outcome of urbanism . . . urbanism apparently has no adverse impact on functions served by kin."[42]

Recent research on immigrant enclaves further undermines the urban-rural duality and offers new insights about assimilation and acculturation in U.S. cities. Since the 1970s, the United States has witnessed a vast new wave of immigration to its large cities. Unlike earlier immigrants, who came mostly from Europe, recent arrivals come largely from Third World countries. Presently, more than half of the population of San Francisco is nonwhite, over one-third of New York City's population is estimated to be foreign born, and the majority of Miami's population is Cuban. Current population trends have led scholars to predict that the ten largest U.S. cities will be more than 50 percent nonwhite within one generation.

Whereas earlier immigrants were, for the most part, unskilled European peasants, today's newcomers are predominantly Latinos and Asians, many of whom are persons of high status. Studies show that while assimilation does occur, "even decades of intergroup contacts have not eventuated in the abandonment of the distinct ethnic identities and social networks."[43] This is because the complex political, economic, and social conditions in today's urban landscape are especially threatening to the most vulnerable immigrants—those who lack professional skills or economic resources. They are thus motivated "to band together around common linguistic and cultural identities in order to influence their life chances and living conditions."[44]

Contrary to assimilation theory, which views ethnic solidarities as impediments to the incorporation of immigrants into the national economic mainstream, recent scholarship shows that group solidarities can provide the necessary insurance that enables impoverished immigrants eventually to launch themselves into the general labor market and to become entrepreneurs.[45] In other words, for individuals who lack either education or wealth, traditional social bonds can provide the moral and material support that contains the otherwise prohibitive risks attendant to participation in the market. Furthermore, it is not unusual for successful second and third generation Americans to preserve ties with ethnic communities because of the special advantages made available to them through such networks.[46]

The arguments presented by Bender, Gans, and Wilson and the recent findings about immigrant life in large U.S. cities provide a formidable challenge to the urban-rural duality that views traditional social relations as the exclusive domain of small towns and rural communities. Indeed, the studies cited above provide massive evidence in support of Bender's claim that rationality and tradition-alism are modes of action that characterize social life in human set-tlements of all sizes. Dualistic thinking has obscured the fact that all social structures are complex combinations of Gemeinschaft and Gesellschaft, and affective relations are therefore always at stake in economic-development policies.

Culture Is Key

The previous section underscores the need for scholars to investi-gate the effects of cultural values on economic development policy making in large cities as well as in small towns. More important, it demonstrates a central tenet of the culturalist school in political science, which posits that trust, predictability, and economy of action are imperatives in *all* individual and collective life because of man's existential powerlessness and limited cognition.[47] These uni-versal human requirements can be met in various ways, such as when individuals maintain kinship bonds, affiliate with religious, ethnic, or minority enclaves, or participate in the civic life of their communities.

The political implications of this argument are twofold. First, by participating in the unique way of life in their particular commu-nities, however defined, individuals "also come to share distinctive values, understandings of social and political realities, and policy preferences."[48] Paying careful attention to the life patterning social structures and cultural values that give security, predictability, character, and meaning to life in a given community may therefore yield a more fine-tuned understanding of local policy responses than urban regime theorists' too narrow focus on "interests" so far has afforded.

A second implication of the cultural argument was articulated by Norton E. Long. It concerns the ways that we think about local communities. Liberal democratic theory and the market model that is derived from it posit an individual who only *consumes* public goods but does not *produce* them, to borrow Long's wry definition.[49] Classical democratic theory, on the other hand, posits an individual whose highest fulfillment is achieved through active citizenship on behalf of the whole commonweal. However, to say that such a "sig-nificant polity" is theoretically possible is not to say that it has recently been realized.[50] To the contrary, Long decried the triviality of politics in U.S. cities and portrayed modern local government leadership as "transient, powerless, and irresponsible."[51] In pondering what conditions might allow a locality to sustain a significant government, he concluded that "the key factor is commitment and the existence of noneconomic grounds for commitment."[52]

Daniel Monti picked up that theme in *Race, Redevelopment, and the New Company Town*, showing that corporations chose to remain in badly deteriorating sections of St. Louis and work in tandem with local government and grassroots neighborhood organizations to rehabilitate those sections, rather than exercise their freedom to relocate to the suburbs as others had done. He concludes that the corporate leaders who spearheaded those efforts were motivated by the civic loyalty that Long spoke of and that their accomplishments issued in a broad public good. The noneconomic grounds for that commitment remain somewhat unclear, however, although family tradition appears to have been a factor in one case. Monti acknowledges that these events were unusual and that there is little evidence to suggest that an attitude of civic responsibility at the corporate level is widespread.

One reason why cities have trivial politics, in Long's view, is the widely accepted fallacy that the contemporary city has "a trivial capacity to affect the important dimensions of the human condition for good or ill."[53] But the poor performance of city governments cannot be explained by a lack of resources or legal powers. The root of the problem lies in our history and national culture, wherein cities have been viewed as little more than "money mining camps" from which, once the lode is used up, the miners "pull up stakes and seek a new lode."[54] The proper role of local government has been viewed as that of facilitator of capital accumulation by private business firms and little more.[55] The problem of ungovernability, in other words, is in our failure to develop a shared conception of a good life in the Aristotelian sense: that is, the enjoyment of locally produced public goods, "appreciated as a good by all precisely because it is shared by all."[56]

We can learn from the culture of ancient Greece, which was strong enough "to create and maintain civic cohesion [that] persisted until Christianity and Islam destroyed it," and we can also learn from "the cities founded by Alexander [that] endured for centuries after the breakup of his empire."[57] These lessons from antiquity teach us that a significant polity requires commitment to a shared way of life that is valued because it endows human life with significance and meaning through participation in a larger, more dignified, and nobler purpose than the egoistic pursuit of material

gain. "Conjoint consumption," even as consumers of sports specta-
cles, does not quite fill the bill. Citizenship means participation in
the *production* of public goods, whatever they may be. For the
ancient Greeks, they were the arts and athletics, among other
things. But the content of the public good matters less than the process of producing it, because for citizens to give of themselves to a
larger goal that is shared by all and thus valued by all is in itself the
highest of all public goods. To be a producer of public goods and not
merely a consumer endows the human personality with self-
respect, respect of others, significance, even nobility. A political
community that engages its citizens in roles that enlarge their dignity and amplify their humanity will instill enduring loyalty and
commitment to that territorially bounded, shared way of life.

In view of the rapidly declining social and economic conditions in U.S. cities, Long poses a question that becomes ever more
pressing: "What are the sources of value that might so infuse a local
turf that its residents would actually struggle to find the means to
remain?"[58] Only by incorporating the cultural variable into our
frameworks for research can we begin to formulate answers to this
urgent question. The chapters that follow present regime analyses
of two communities that no longer enjoyed the same vibrant economic base that they once did, but where black and white, rich and
poor continued their struggle to create a good life together in the
same place anyway, because community still mattered. It was in the
process of discovering the different ways that these communities
afforded noneconomic grounds for commitment that I was led to
this theoretical synthesis.

CONCLUSION

One of the strengths of the political economy approach to the
study of local communities is its ability to accommodate variation
and complexity within a broad, general framework. In explaining
that variation, different contributors to the regime paradigm have
emphasized different variables as important determinants of economic policy decisions. Additionally, "what is important in regime
theory is the ruling coalition, the winners and losers, the prevailing
pattern of public policy. Behind the formal rules that govern the economic and political system, behind the prevailing political style, are
informal arrangements for governing the city based on a dominant
coalition that decides policy and articulates a vision for the city,"

according to Swanstrom.[59] For Logan and Molotch, that coalition is a growth machine. Its vision for the city is economic opportunity and prosperity for the many; its reality is a money-making apparatus for the few. But any number of regime types is theoretically possible, and proper classification requires attention to the kind of leadership that is exercised and the normative values it upholds.

Proponents of regime theory and the growth machine thesis agree that development policy is not economically determined as the market model posits, but instead grows out of real choices that localities make through the political process.[60] The theoretical synthesis presented here can contribute a fuller and more practical understanding of the role that culture plays in that process. The case studies that follow, by closely analyzing the unique way of life in two communities, expose the contextual character of economic rationality and, at the same time, reveal a range of noneconomic values that have so infused the local turf that its policies cannot be understood apart from them. Finally, this work demonstrates that economic development is no mere technical matter to be understood, planned, executed, and interpreted to laypersons by policy experts acting in quiet collusion with public and private elites, for it is, in the fullest sense of the word, a *community* process.

3

A HISTORY OF SOMERSET COUNTY

This chapter does not purport to offer a complete or even a rounded history of Somerset County. Instead, it highlights events of a particular kind. It focuses on instigating events because of their structure-altering potential. The following pages provide a historical account of how a planter's regime came into being in the northern part of Somerset County at the close of the seventeenth century and how a different regime evolved in the city of Crisfield and other maritime communities bordering the Chesapeake Bay. The narrative explains how particular cultures and social structures became like fixed frameworks during colonial times, thereafter shaping and reshaping the distinctive ways of life in these localities throughout three centuries. It also reports what occurred when those structures were threatened.

From the American Revolution onward, the traditional way of life in Somerset was periodically buffeted by instigating events, including political challenges, legal attacks, state and federal intervention, ecological disasters, social movements, electoral uprisings, cultural invasion, global economic forces, and outright war. Keeping in mind that structures can be explained in terms of an interaction between the desirability of their consequences for different groups and the relative power of those groups, we will see that whether these disruptions were viewed as threats to be resisted and overcome or as harbingers of salutary change depended upon one's place in the social order.

The history of these events will make apparent who has benefited most (and who least) from the prevailing way of life in these communities. It will show how different elements in the community responded when their way of life was challenged and what kinds of resources they brought into the struggle. The examination of how the dominant regime in particular responded to instigating events and the adaptations that it made to contextual change will reveal how *semper eadem* (ever the same) became the chosen policy, as well as the official motto, in Somerset County.

One consequence of selecting events of this kind and then telescoping them into a single chapter is to dramatize some of the least savory aspects of Somerset's history. While the overall picture may not therefore appear balanced, it nonetheless faithfully describes the historical processes that are germane to this inquiry. Social structures usually support established power, and power is rarely relinquished gracefully. A different research question might have produced a more celebratory account.

The great political scientist V. O. Key, Jr., observed that "it is impossible to speculate on the nature of political behavior without attributing to events long past their profound influence in the establishment of current habits of action."[1] Thus the history of these events, the struggles precipitated by them, and their outcomes inform our understanding of the way of life in Princess Anne and Crisfield in the recent era. Bringing to light the social structures and social processes long at work in Somerset County sets the stage for the two case studies that follow.

HARVESTERS OF LAND AND WATER

Maryland's Eastern Shore was colonized in the early seventeenth century, and in the beginning opportunity abounded for settlers from all walks of life. By 1637, tobacco had become such a booming export industry that the land surrounding the Chesapeake Bay was almost everywhere snatched up for tobacco cultivation by enterprising Englishmen. One exception was the remote and low-lying country later to be known as Somerset, where the land was the least productive in all of the vicinity. Of Somerset's 611 square miles, 46 percent is under water, and much of the rest is beach and tidal marsh.[2] Another large portion was heavily forested in colonial times. It is estimated that only a fifth of the county could ever have produced high yields of tobacco, and because the soil was a sandy loam, the crops were of the lowest and least remunerative grade.[3] An early English tobacco factor described the land as full of "convicts, bugs, mosquitoes, worms of every sort both land and water, spiders, snakes, hornets, wasps, sea nettles, ticks, gnats, thunder and lightening, excessive heat, excessive cold, and other irregularities in abundance."[4]

The above irregularities notwithstanding, Somerset was eventually settled by religious and political dissidents from Virginia, pirates, runaway servants, and escaping convicts and slaves.[5] The dissidents were, by and large, persons of means who acquired arable land in the north of the county by grant, planted it in tobacco and other crops, and procured servants as they were able. People in the fugitive category settled along the numerous inlets, creeks, bays, and subestuaries that lace the shoreline and harvested the bay for their subsistence. They were called "watermen," a Middle English word used in the Chesapeake region to distinguish those who lacked the resources to acquire land.[6]

Evidently the distinction is still sharp, for there is today a deep social cleavage between members of the water-based fishing community in the southwest of the county and the land-based agricultural community in the north. An observer reports that dating and marrying across this line elicits opprobrium. "It's akin to a prejudice," said another: "It has to do with the kind of people they are." Thus Somerset County was, from the beginning, composed of two quite different, mutually antagonistic sectors. "North county" and "south county" have preserved their differences and rivalries into the present.

Each of the two sectors has its own commercial center and outlying villages. Princess Anne, the county seat, is the center of commerce for the declining agricultural industry. Incorporated in 1733, it is a quaint, historic inland village, situated near Somerset's northern border. The lesser farming villages, such as Westover and Mt. Vernon, often contain hardly more than a church or two and a single general store.

From the southwestern edge of the county, the city of Crisfield spills over into Tangier Sound. It is the commercial center for the dying seafood industry. Having always harvested the bay for their subsistence, many of the residents of this blue-collar, maritime community are as much at home on the water as on the land. There is a sprinkling of remote fishing settlements along the county's 619 miles of jagged shoreline: Dames Quarter, Deal Island, Frenchtown, Fairmont, Rumbley, and Chance.[7] And nine miles west of the Crisfield city dock lies Smith Island, the most isolated refuge of the watermen, where the Methodist church functions as the local government and English is spoken with an Elizabethan twang.[8]

FIGURE 3.1 Crisfield City Dock

Those who "follow the water" for their livelihood, and also the "growers," are today almost exclusively of Anglo-Saxon descent, but there was a time when significant numbers of watermen and farmers were black. Somerset historically has had a large population of free blacks whose forebears migrated north from Virginia in colonial times. Many were entrepreneurial, upwardly mobile, and prosperous. In 1860, slaves constituted little more than half of the county's black population, and the remaining 4,483 black Americans earned their living as independent farmers, tradesmen, and laborers.[9]

Even though Maryland is considered a border state, Somerset could technically be classified as a black belt county, because African Americans today constitute 38 percent of the population.[10] As in similar counties in the Deep South, the historic institution of slavery and its aftermath have left their stain of bigotry and continuing racial descrimination in the culture and social practice of the white population and widespread economic dependency and resentment among blacks.

There is a stable black middle class in the county consisting of educators in the public school system and in the historically black University of Maryland Eastern Shore (UMES), which is located just outside of Princess Anne. Middle-class blacks also travel to professional and managerial jobs outside of the county. Unemployment is high in the black working class, but many laborers, especially women, find seasonal work in the seafood processing plants in Crisfield and its environs. Finally, there is a small community of black yeomen farmers that is concentrated in Marion which lies between Crisfield and Princess Anne. It is from this group that the managerial and professional class largely springs. As with the white population, many local blacks are tenth generation Americans whose ancestry can be traced back to seventeenth-century colonial settlers, including free blacks, whites, and African slaves.

THE PLANTERS' REGIME

The rise of the planters' regime in Somerset County, and indeed throughout the whole Chesapeake region, resulted from various factors, but the most important of these was the relationship between the tobacco economy and slaves. A great many of Maryland's first settlers arrived as indentured servants, and those who survived to complete their terms of service eventually acquired land and servants of their own. Because of the high price of tobacco, they often became prosperous as freedmen, and social relations were characterized by a rough equality.

There were structural changes after 1680, however, which permanently altered this homogeneity and created an increasingly hierarchical society in the Chesapeake.[11] The price of tobacco began to decline after 1620, and by 1680 profits had fallen off so badly that freed servants found it increasingly difficult to buy land. Diminishing opportunities in the colony greatly reduced the stream of white immigrants, with the result that the demand for slaves was greatly increased. The labor market of indentured servants was thus replaced by a great wave of African slaves that poured into the region in the 1690s, and from that time on, "sons of poor men rarely procured land or unfree labor; sons of men of substance usually replicated the status of their fathers."[12] The formation of political dynasties, or "courthouse gangs," was a parallel process, with sons succeeding their fathers in the General Assembly and as justices of the peace in colonial courts.[13] Thus a sharp decline in the price of tobacco and a subsequent rise in the price of slaves gave birth to what amounted to a hereditary aristocracy based upon extensive landholdings and control of a self-replicating labor force.

FIGURE 3.2 Princess Anne's Historic Teakle Mansion

The American Revolution

When the American Revolution came, some viewed it as a threat to the planter's dominance. This conservative sentiment was voiced by the last proprietary governor, who was afraid that "all power is getting fast into the hands of the very lowest people."[14] His words reflected a widespread concern among landed elites that the democratic and egalitarian ideals of the Revolution might be realized and thus disrupt the established social order that was based upon political and material inequality and special privilege. What happened instead was that an oligarchy composed of men of hereditary wealth and social standing was able quickly to secure its control of the government by inserting stipulations in the Maryland Constitution of 1776 that provided large property holders with cumulative advantages.[15]

Somerset's watermen sided with the British during this conflict "because of their hatred for Maryland's slave-holding rebel gentry. Many poor watermen had been humiliated by arrogant planters who treated them worse than slaves."[16] Revolts against the revolutionary government were frequently fomented by Tory watermen in the maritime communities of the Chesapeake during the war, but in the years that followed, the landed elites consolidated their control.[17]

The hegemony of the large planters was thus firmly established both at county and at state levels in the aftermath of the American Revolution, constituting a landed white male oligarchy, or planter's regime. This governing structure was shaken but not dislodged by the collapse of the tobacco market in 1820, which precipitated an economic decline throughout the region.[18] It was not until the Civil War that the next serious challenge to the planter's regime occurred.

In summary, the decline of white servitude and the prohibitive price of slaves placed a premium on inheritance as a means of accumulating wealth. This created a highly stratified agricultural economy in the Chesapeake region wherein the great majority of white planters owned small family farms and relied upon the labor of their families, one or two slaves, and an occasional white hired hand, while a privileged minority operated large plantations with many slaves.[19] Thus a caste and class society was formed in which a landed elite commanded deference from blacks, yeomen, poor whites, women, and children. The founding of the new nation raised hopes (and fears) that a democratic regime would establish itself in place of the courthouse gangs. But "the egalitarian impulses of the Revolutionary era were finally overcome," and the planters' oligarchy continued to dominate the counties and the state legislature for over two hundred years.[20] Meanwhile, the independent watermen of the Chesapeake and their kin lived defiantly apart from the social and political order that prevailed on the mainland.[21]

The Civil War

The agricultural oligarchies of the Eastern Shore and of Southern Maryland were again threatened during the Civil War when the state Democratic party was virtually outlawed as seditious by federal authorities. At the start of the war, Maryland was almost equally divided on the question of secession, with Unionist sentiment prevailing in the north and west of the state, and strong Southern sympathies predominating in the Eastern Shore and Southern Maryland. The watermen, apparently ambivalent about their allegiances during this struggle, "professed loyalty to the union," while enjoying "a thriving illegal commerce with the Confederacy."[22] The state was thus wavering on the question of secession, and some historians argue that it was the Federal military force in the end that kept Maryland in the Union.[23]

In 1861, the newly formed Union party gained control of the state with a platform that opposed abolition as well as secession. Slaves in Maryland and the other border states found easy refuge in neighboring free jurisdictions, however, and the Union army conscripted all the slaves it could entice. With the institution of slavery thus undermined, a rapid shift in sentiment toward emancipation occurred throughout the state. Changes in the national political environment had altered opportunity structures for enslaved blacks and changed the worldview of Marylanders on the whole.[24] The "Unconditional Unionists" then advanced the cause of emancipation by appealing to the economic and class interests of yeomen and poor whites, and called for a constitutional convention in 1864.

Reacting finally to their loss of political dominance, the Democrats rebounded under the leadership of Oden Bowie, a Southern Maryland tobacco planter. But they were unable to reassert their power in sufficient time or force to prevent ratification of the 1864 state constitution, which abolished slavery in Maryland and changed the basis of representation in the state legislature such that power was shifted away from the southern counties to the northern and western sections which were Unionist strongholds.

By 1867, however, the recently victorious Union party lay in ruins. It had foundered on an internal schism over the question of universal manhood suffrage, which the white male voters in Maryland overwhelmingly opposed.[25] The "Conservative Unionists" were reabsorbed into the Democratic party and all was forgiven, while the "Radical Unionists" continued to advocate suffrage for blacks and began to regroup as the nucleus of the emerging Republican party. The Democrats had gained enough strength by 1867 to ratify a new state constitution by a two-to-one margin.

The constitution of 1867 made no provision for the enfranchisement of blacks, and it reinstated the prewar basis of representation in the state legislature, which was calculated on total population instead of the white population only. "Thus the voteless Negro was used to increase the power of the southern and Eastern Shore counties where the Democratic party was strong."[26] In 1870, the Fifteenth Amendment gave the vote to blacks without Maryland's ratification.

After the Civil War, former slaveholders retained their land, and slaveholding was replaced by tenancy, sharecropping, and debt peonage—structures that approximated the state of slavery insofar as possible, short of outright property in persons.[27] These structural adjustments were reinforced by measures so Draconian that they instilled enduring taboos in the local culture. Black aspirations, breaches of white caste loyalty, and political insurgency by members of either race met with violent sanctions. Arsonists, for example, destroyed eleven schools established for blacks in Baltimore, Cecil, Kent, Queen Anne's, and Somerset counties after the Civil War.[28]

Political Insurgency

The planter's regime suffered another blow in the state election of 1895, when the Democratic party in Maryland became divided over allegations of corruption and internal mismanagement. Riding the crest of a statewide bi-partisan reform movement, the Republican party successfully combined with black voters to capture virtually every key elective office in Maryland. Once in office, however, the Republicans defaulted on their campaign promises to blacks and thus provoked a backlash among black voters that enabled the Democrats to rally.

While Democratic planters in Maryland were smarting from their electoral defeat of 1895, the Populist uprising was engendering the wrath of large planters in black belt counties throughout the South. Thus when Maryland planters tightened their political control in the state legislature after 1900, the virulent disfranchisement movement which they launched against blacks merged with the larger repressive movement that was sweeping the South.[29] While the planters ultimately failed in their efforts to pass constitutional amendments that would deny blacks their right to vote, they nevertheless stirred up such a poisonous cauldron of racial hatred that there are communities in Southern Maryland and the Eastern Shore that have yet to recover from the debilitating aftermath.[30]

One of the first effects of the inflamed climate was a great increase in informal segregation followed by the passage of laws in 1904 and 1908 that were "designed to fix the negro 'in his place' for all eternity."[31] This formidable structure of Jim Crow laws instituted segregation in every aspect of public life and renewed the historic assault on black education, leaving a legacy of severely handicapped black Americans and entrenched social problems that continue to confound rural reformers throughout the southern region.[32]

During this period, the city of Crisfield, among others, became "so impatient with the state's necessity to amend its Constitution before barring Negroes from the polls and its seeming inability to secure such amendment" that in 1904 it wrote disenfranchising provisions into the city charter. They remained in effect for six years until they were ruled unconstitutional by the U.S. Supreme Court.[33]

If the upset election of 1895 was the precipitating cause of renewed repression by the planter's regime in Maryland, the mindset and motives that inspired these measures were consistent with the culture of the larger plantation region. By making white supremacy the central issue in Southern politics, the white planters aimed to secure their own political ascendance in perpetuity by insuring that whites could never again join forces with black Republicans to defeat the conservative Democratic party in the South.[34]

The Attorney General's Quest

Violence was the chosen means for maintaining blacks in submission during slavery and afterwards. The institution of slavery was, in Cash's words, "the very school of violence."[35] But just as the institution of slavery had transgressed against the dominant American ethos in the nineteenth century, the Southern culture of extra-legal violence was antagonistic to the dominant values in the United States in the twentieth century.[36] Perhaps it was inevitable, then, that the counties of the lower Eastern Shore sooner or later would come into open confrontation with state authorities over the crimes of violence that were being committed against blacks with evident impunity in these localities.[37]

Between 1889 and 1918, there were twelve lynchings of blacks in the counties of the Eastern Shore and Southern Maryland, one of which occurred in Princess Anne and another in Crisfield.[38] A new spate of violence started with the onset of the Great Depression when blacks increased their outmigration.[39] In 1931 there were two lynchings in Somerset's neighboring counties of Wicomico and Worcester, and in 1933 Princess Anne became the site of the last lynching reported in Maryland. These events fueled growing outrage in the state and in the nation. A classic study of Southern lynching explains:

> the damage done to labor conditions, investment of capital, reputation of the community, and the like is inestimable. The lynchings focused attention on these communities, not as places where labor conditions are settled and life and property are safe, but rather as places where human relations are unstable and life and property are subject to the whims of a mob. Every lynching gives unfavorable publicity not only to the immediate community involved, but to the whole section.[40]

The nation's reaction to the lynching in Wicomico County illustrates the point. Public and private organizations were stirred to publicize and protest these crimes while calling for justice. The outspoken H. L. Mencken, writing for *Baltimore Sun*, characterized the lower Eastern Shore as a civilization "wherein there are no competent police, little save a simian self-seeking in public office, no apparent intelligence on the bench, and no courage and decency in the local press."[41]

While resentment over the lynchings in Worcester and Wicomico was still smoldering, the crime in Princess Anne set off a firestorm of condemnation that swept the country. The Maryland attorney general, William Preston Lane, was especially incensed, and he vowed to bring the Princess Anne killers to justice and put an end to lynching in the state. His passionate quest became a national *cause celebre*.

In an unpublished history entitled *Tidewater Somerset: 1850–1970*, which was first commissioned and then suppressed by a local historical society, Wennersten provides a detailed account of the state's last lynching. The condensed version presented here conveys the essential facts. On October 18, 1933, George Armwood, a mentally retarded black youth, was awaiting trial in the Princess Anne jail. The sheriff earlier had removed him to Baltimore to insure his safety, but First Circuit Court Judge Robert F. Duer, acting out of a misguided deference to local sentiment, insisted that the prisoner be returned to Princess Anne. The charges against Armwood were that he had accosted a white woman, intending to rob her, and in the ensuing scuffle had damaged her dress.

FIGURE 3.3 The Jailhouse from Which George Armwood Was Abducted

As night fell, a crowd gathered at the jail, tensions grew, and a riot ensued. At nine o'clock a mob broke into the jail with battering rams, seized Armwood, and dragged him to Judge Duer's house. While the judge entertained dinner guests inside of his Princess Anne residence, Armwood was beaten, hanged, dismembered, and burned on the spacious front lawn. Potential witnesses to the crime were many, for it was reported that these acts were committed in the midst of "a cheering crowd" estimated to be "about 5,000 men."[42] Those who were known to be responsible for Armwood's murder were detained by the sheriff, then freed by Judge Duer.

So great was the attorney general's disgust and indignation at the crime against Armwood and the ensuing miscarriage of justice that he had the names of the perpetrators and the evidence against them read into the *Congressional Record* while testifying for a federal anti-lynching law.[43] In attempting to put an end to lynching in

Somerset County and Maryland, Lane pursued every legal instrument at his command, but he nevertheless failed to secure a single conviction in the Armwood case.

This event illustrates the power and tenacity of the culture that deemed it acceptable to keep the Negro "in his place" at any social, moral, or economic cost, and to exonerate and protect those who committed the mayhem. Lynching was intended to prevent the outmigration of blacks from rural areas.[44] It also served as a socializing force within the white caste, reinforcing what Cash calls the "ancient pattern": the mindset of white caste solidarity in the cause of racial hatred and Southern patriotism.[45] The atrocity that was committed in Princess Anne and its coverup are indicative of the kind of structures and culture that were established by the large, slaveholding class of planters there and elsewhere in the plantation South.[46]

Princess Anne was the home of a planter's regime that was based upon the exploitation of a captive labor force and most firmly committed, as we have seen, to preserving its economic and political dominance at any price.[47] Preston Lane challenged the way of life there, and he lost. The attorney general could not have known in his hour of defeat that his efforts had furthered a much larger cause.

The Civil Rights Movement

The long view of history sometimes reveals what is hid in the present. Contemporary observers were unaware that the lynching of George Armwood had already ignited the spiritual torch that Maryland would carry into the frontrunner's place in the civil rights movement. As a border state that is divided by four geographical regions, each with different and mutually antagonistic cultures, Maryland was in a unique position to serve in this leadership role.[48] The heinousness of the crimes on the Eastern Shore, the predictable abortions of justice that followed, and the publicity that the outraged attorney general brought to these cases all worked to galvanize longstanding ire in the rest of the state and a moral commitment to bring about change.

In the 1930s, Baltimore was the home of the nation's strongest black newspaper, the *Afro-American*. Responding to the tragic events on the Eastern Shore, and especially in Princess Anne, the newspaper called for revitalization of the Baltimore chapter of the National Association for the Advancement of Colored People

(NAACP), which had long been inactive. The editors also persuaded the NAACP to appoint Lillie May Jackson to serve as its head. She was an inspired visionary and a bold leader, and she soon locked horns with the cautious intellectuals on her board. In time, educators and preachers were replaced with longshoremen and labor leaders.[49]

Jackson was deeply religious, passionate, upright, and utterly unbending in her demands for equality and justice for African Americans under the law in Maryland.[50] She inspired and attracted many people, black and white, to the cause. Under her leadership, the Baltimore NAACP grew to more than twenty thousand members after World War II. She was continuously allied with the black churches and the *Afro-American*, prompting the historian George H. Callcott to name them "the triple generals in the crusade—the three avenues of protest—for the Maryland civil rights movement."[51]

From the mid-1930s forward, the role of Marylanders in the national civil rights movement can hardly be overstated. This sketch cannot do justice to the range of reforms that resulted from the joined efforts of black and white leaders and common people during this period, leading the nation. In 1935, a young lawyer from Baltimore, Thurgood Marshall, argued a case for the Baltimore NAACP that won the admission of the first black student to the University of Maryland Law School, where Marshall himself had been denied admission five years earlier.

While Marshall went on to win equal pay for black teachers in county after county in Maryland during the thirties, Jackson and the *Afro-American* together persuaded blacks that their greatest strength was through voting and alliance with trusted officials. Thus when Theodore Roosevelt McKeldin became mayor of Baltimore in 1943 and governor of Maryland in 1950, he won these elections by the margin that black voters gave him.[52]

Mayor McKeldin's accomplishments on behalf of Baltimore's black residents are listed by Callcott:

McKeldin appointed blacks to almost all city boards: education, health, recreation, planning, and the rest. He ordered city employment of blacks, notably as police officers, librarians, and nurses. He worked with the federal government to obtain additional black housing, with the Urban League to find private employers for blacks, with the unions to promote acceptance of black workers, and with the NAACP to persuade the local press, notably the *Sunpapers*, to soften their emphasis on racial crime and expand their coverage of black achievement.[53]

While McKeldin was governor, Maryland became the first legally segregated state to accept the Supreme Court's school desegregation order. The *Brown v. Board of Education* decision was handed down on May 5, 1954, ordering all schools to begin integration within one year. According to Callcott's account,

> That evening Jackson and her friends celebrated with lemonade and cookies, proud that one of their own, Thurgood Marshall, had been the landmark case's chief attorney. The next day Governor McKeldin and Mayor D'Alesandro issued statements hailing the decision and promising to uphold the law. A week later [Baltimore school] Superintendent Fischer called the school board into session and gave them a carefully prepared plan for compliance, not for 1955, as required, but for the fall of 1954. . . . On June 3 the board voted unanimously to proceed. The following day the Catholic archbishop announced that the state's Catholic schools would voluntarily comply, and two weeks after that the University of Maryland announced it would accept undergraduate blacks to its classes and dormitories.[54]

Callcott identifies not only the *Brown* decision but also Baltimore's response to it as the events that brought blacks and sympathetic whites to the very apogee of hope for the whole nation in their struggle for racial equality and justice. "The quiet hope of an oppressed people was about to burst forth into a crusade."[55]

The triumphs and vicissitudes of the national civil rights movement are extensively documented elsewhere; there is no need to recount them here. Suffice it to say that Maryland continued to lead on a number of fronts. In 1963, for example, Governor Tawes introduced a public accommodations bill that passed in the Maryland General Assembly, but not before Lower Shore delegates amended it to exempt their own region. In 1964, the legislature extended the law to include the whole state—three months in advance of the national civil rights act. Maryland's open housing act came one year ahead of the new federal law.[56] Governor Tawes himself was a native of Crisfield, which makes these achievements seem all the more striking.

Tawes' Eastern Shore constituents were less sanguine than he was about social change. By 1963, the movement had come home to the place where, in a sense, it had started thirty years earlier, catalyzed by the Eastern Shore lynchings. The fiery speech by H. Rap Brown and the conflagration that destroyed much of Cambridge, the Dorchester County seat, in the first urban riot were extensively covered by the national news media at the time. But the demonstrations and riots that occurred the following year in Princess Anne are less widely known.

Founded as the Princess Anne Academy, a Methodist school for blacks, in the nineteenth century, the University of Maryland Eastern Shore (UMES) became a federally supported land grant college in 1890. It was located on the outskirts of Princess Anne, where, according to one of its presidents, the school had always been "imprisoned by an invisible wall of racism."[57] In 1964, the college came into open conflict with the town.

We have seen that the Lower Shore counties had gained an exemption from the state's 1963 public accommodations law and that the exemption was overturned by the state legislature early in 1964. In February of that year, inspired by the spreading civil rights activism of black students elsewhere, students at UMES organized a march into Princess Anne to test the town's restaurants for service. Worried town commissioners appointed a biracial commission to negotiate student demands. The commission's head, white attorney Alexander Jones, confessed that racial attitudes in Princess Anne were "more like Mississippi than the rest of Maryland," and tensions grew.[58] Burning crosses appeared on the campus, beatings occurred, and state troopers patrolled. The students were unyielding, and political leaders were silent. In this charged atmosphere, people were frightened. "The town commissioners wired Governor Tawes to send in the National Guard."[59]

Then on February 26, Gloria Richardson, the brilliant and angry black leader who, with H. Rap Brown, had stirred racial conflict in Cambridge the previous year, led a march from the campus, up the hill, and into the town. There the marchers were set upon by white hoodlums, dogs, and police wielding fire hoses in an attack so vicious that sixty students were hospitalized.[60] Wennersten reports that seventy-five students sang "We Are Soldiers in the Army" as they marched into Princess Anne again the next day.[61]

The contrast between Baltimore in 1954 and Princess Anne in 1964 could hardly have been more stark. Within one decade, Maryland offered the nation a beacon of hope for the national civil rights movement and unforgettable visions of violence and racial hatred. On racial issues, if ever there was "a house divided against itself," it was Maryland.

School integration was another point of contention in Somerset County. The "freedom of choice" plan that the county adopted failed so completely that in 1964, ten years after *Brown*, only nineteen black students attended white schools.[62] Somerset County alone in the state lost its federal funds for failure even to have an acceptable plan. The result of the federal ultimatum was that in 1969, fifteen years after the Baltimore schools were integrated, Somerset finally complied with the law.[63] School integration has not meant all that its advocates hoped it would mean for black children. In the last year before integration took place, there were eleven black principals in the Somerset County school system. But in 1991, twenty-two years later, there was not one. Black children reported that they were not treated fairly by teachers and principals in academic or disciplinary matters. The rate of expulsion for blacks was especially high, and the local NAACP chapter was looking into it.

One apparent advance was the appointment of an African American, Dwayne Whittington, Jr., to serve as the superintendent of schools. But Whittington's detractors in the black community claimed that he was the prototype of what, in the local vernacular, were called "system blacks." These were people whose role was to still racial protest by legitimating "the system." In exchange, they were recruited to high positions and even lionized by the white ruling group. When Whittington was questioned, as he frequently was, about the disproportionally high rate of expulsion of black students, the superintendent's usual reply was that because he personally reviewed every expulsion that occurred in the county school system, and because he was black, "racism could not be a factor."[64]

However, Whittington's view of local race relations changed, when, in 1993, the county's all-white school board suddenly replaced him without explanation. I have been told that after a prolonged period of emotional and spiritual anguish, the former superintendent emerged from his ordeal as a new man. Black citizens speculated that he might have been waylaid, as it were, "on the road to Damascus," for he who had been "too arrogant even to listen to his own pastor" became humble, cooperative, and a dedicated worker for the betterment of the black community.[65]

This research did not produce clear evidence of self-conscious efforts to block the educational and economic advancement of blacks in the recent era, nor would the evidence support an opposing claim. What was clear, however, and prevalent to a disheartening degree was the entrenched racism still infusing the culture. In 1991, whites could still regale one another in public, without apprehension of disapproval, about "the time back in '64 when ole Bate Williamson hosed the niggers down the hill and state troopers sicked 'em with K9 dogs." [66] Mimicking African American dialects could still be counted on to evoke amusement at white social gatherings. Sadly, even some outsiders who had moved into the county seemed to take on this mindset after a few years in residence. One supposes that the untenable status of "foreigner" exerts great psychological pressure to conform. Individuals and groups require trust in social relations, and among the white residents of Somerset County, trust is still predicated upon regular demonstrations of white caste loyalty.

The civil rights movement brought racial equality under the law, but the subtler forms of discrimination continued. Racial stereotypes and taboos embedded in culture cannot be eradicated by votes in the State House or Congress, or expunged by Supreme Court decisions, although the legal achievements of the civil rights movement brought critically important advances in racial justice that should never be minimized. If courageous moral leadership had also been demonstrated by the local newspapers and white people's churches, it might have inspired the people to attain to new cultural and spiritual values, but too often these influential institutions instead served to reinforce the status quo.

THE BURDEN OF SOMERSET'S HISTORY

If there has been one overriding theme that has guided the peculiar mode of development in Somerset, as elsewhere in the plantation South, it has been the planter class's commitment, not to the maximization of its economic return, but to the preservation of its economic and political dominance at any cost.[67] Thus the political economy of these communities was significantly conditioned by the particular path of institutional and cultural development that distinguished the slaveholding South from the northern colonies.[68] We have seen that local institutions have sometimes been forced to adapt to external pressure for social change, but adaptations were made always with a view to the maintenance of local traditions.

Historically, the assured supply of cheap labor militated against the mechanization and modernization of agriculture here as in other plantation regions.[69] Black belt landlords throughout the plantation South opposed thoroughgoing industrialization and created impediments to the realization of business interests that would threaten their supply of cheap labor.[70] Competition for labor has been discouraged by large planters and seafood packers in Somerset County up to the present era. In the words of one informant, "The powers that be—the handful of people who run things in the county—they won't let anything change. General Motors tried to locate here in the 1950s. Later we lost a Dupont plant. It used to be the seafood people, but now it's the farmers. They don't want anybody bringing in the minimum wage."

Economist Gavin Wright has argued that slavery was detrimental to the South because it fostered a reliance on labor-intensive, resource-extractive export industries, which expand rapidly during periods of rising external demand but which do not lay the institutional foundations for sustained growth once this era has passed.[71] Because the soil in Somerset was relatively poor for tobacco production, farmers there had diversified early by planting vegetables and fruits and developing crafts industries such as smithing and tanning.[72] They were therefore protected from complete economic failure when the collapse of the tobacco market came and were able to maintain a sometimes secondary but always influential role in the county's regime throughout the one-hundred-year rise and decline of the county's seafood industry.

Somerset's large, slaveholding planters had gained control of the polity and the economy by the end of the Revolution, and over the centuries they surmounted many challenges to their ascendancy. But in 1962, the Supreme Court's *Baker v. Carr* decision ordered reapportionment on the basis of "one man, one vote," thus ending the rural elite's political control of the state. Although the economic, political, and legal bases of their dominance have seriously eroded, their influence is still felt locally in the present era. The planters' regime, and especially the slavery that was the source of its influence in the region, has left its legacy of racism, poverty, ignorance, and economic dependency. The antidemocratic values that it embraced lie deep in the culture.

There is an insidious moral pathology that infuses the mindset of a people in the aftermath of mob violence of the kind that Somerset County more than once witnessed: pervasive dishonesty, citizenship debased, ethical standards lowered. Leading citizens are compromised, and "barbarism and deception are translated into virtues."[73] John Dollard, in a brilliant psychoanalytic study of a small Southern city, identified a characteristic psychological system organized around a set of what he calls the "defensive beliefs" of the dominant caste.[74] Gunner Myrdal likewise described some of its features.[75] This defensive belief system, the alibi system, refers to the set of externalizations, projections, fantasies, denial, and other distortions of reality that serve to rationalize and justify barbarian acts and a way of life based upon racial dominance and subordination. It is what W. J. Cash, in his 1941 title, refers to as *The Mind of the South.*

John Shelton Reed's research has verified the existence of a distinctive Southern culture that is given to the indulgence of private violence, and he challenges the conventional wisdom that it vanished with the end of racial segregation and the coming of a "new South."[76] The Southern mindset was easy to observe in many white informants during this research. And the readiness of whites to disparage the black population as unreliable and "lacking the work ethic" ill served the purposes of that sector of the community that was trying to attract outside industry, jobs, and capital into the county. It did, however, serve to excuse the withholding of benefits and the minimum wage. Variations of the racist alibi system were continuously promulgated in Somerset, with the effect that the impoverishment and dependency of much of the labor force was perpetuated, and the farmers and seafood packers were able, even through very hard times, to maintain their hold. We have seen how these elements responded when traditional structures were jeopardized by instigating events.

THE MORAL ECONOMY OF THE WATERMEN[77]

The watermen's community encompassing Crisfield and its environs is based in a different economy, a different politics, and a different culture. Watermen jealously guard their independence, and they have never sought assimilation with the dominant culture that prevails further inland. Typically proud, humorous, insouciant, and defiant, they remain, as one Eastern Shore observer said, "a people unto themselves."

It is generally acknowledged that the Picaroons were the first colonial inhabitants of Somerset County. According to legend, the towns were teeming with pirates, who "just moved onto a piece of high land near the water and defied anyone to impose authority over them."[78] They lived by fishing and trapping, raiding the ships in the bay, and occasionally plundering other settlements. As time went on, the Picaroons were joined by escapees of various descriptions. If there is one thing these fugitives all had in common, it was that

FIGURE 3.4 Smith Island

they found on the water the means of subsistence that gave them their freedom, albeit outside of the law.

The spirit of the Picaroons is alive today in the culture of the watermen, who are law abiding only after a fashion. Following their mass conversion to Methodism in the early nineteenth century, most of them devoutly conformed to new religious and moral standards within their own communities. But watermen remain stalwartly defiant of external authority, even to the point, in the case of

Smith Islanders, of refusing to obtain license tags for their cars. In their view, the ultimate degradations are to be forced to sell their labor to other persons for wages and to submit to external restrictions on what they see as their God-given right to harvest the bay.[79]

"Commodification of labor" has not yet occurred among the watermen of the Chesapeake. As for their attitude toward regulation, the following episode reported by Warner conveys their perspective:

> Having outlined certain conservation measures, he (the head of Maryland's Department of Natural Resources) asked for discussion. After a silence, a rugged young islander rose to his feet. "Mr. Manning, there is something you don't understand," the young waterman said. "These here communities on the Shore, our little towns on the island and over to mainland, was all founded on the right of free plunder. If you follow the water, that's how it was and that's how it's got to be." Manning gave up the discussion period. The Picaroons would have cheered.[80]

There is a historical and cultural continuity in Somerset's fishing society that continues to shape economic and political choices up to the present. "There's a veneer of Christianity," observed one informant, "but underneath there's a willingness to do whatever it takes to survive." Survival has not been easy for watermen and their families at any time in their history, and the means of securing it are preserved in the local traditions and values.

Christian mores are often compatible with the survival ethos in this preindustrial context; it is only in a full-fledged market society that rationality appears to conflict with the brotherhood of man. A noncompetitive, communitarian ethos is deeply ingrained in the culture of Smith Islanders. It is continuously nourished by the Methodist church that is the social, political, and spiritual center of island life, and it is manifest in Somerset's other fishing communities also. People who practice self-reliance upon the high seas do not last long. Fishermen, like mountain climbers, trust each other daily with their lives.[81] The oysterman's existential powerlessness in the face of the forces of nature and his vulnerability before events that are beyond his ken or control render him needful of relationships with others upon whom he can surely rely.

Even in the city of Crisfield, which is a commercial center, economic maximization is not always the prevailing principle. In fact, the competitive materialism that it implies has historically been viewed as a threat to the solidarity of the community on which each person's individual survival is seen to depend. Here, social status has not been predicated upon material wealth. To the contrary, it has traditionally been frowned upon to take home a larger catch than, or to display material superiority to one's neighbor.[82] The leveling ethos prevents the growth of severe class cleavages, protects the solidarity of the community, and, by spreading risk in a marginal subsistence economy, it tries to guarantee that everyone will pull through.

The Invasion of the Drudgers

If egalitarian and communitarian values are compatible with the community's survival ethos, then isolationism and protectionism are the other side of the coin, and there is reason to suppose that these cultural traits were forged in the furnace of historical experience. Until the mid nineteenth century, the Chesapeake was an isolated and unspoiled natural oasis, prodigal in its abundance of crustaceans, fish, and waterfowl. But the tranquility of the region was suddenly shattered when the railroad came to Crisfield after the Civil War and catapulted the city into an oystering boom.

The laying of the first railroad tracks from the port city of Baltimore to the cities in the northeast and midwest opened up vast new markets for the delicacies of the Chesapeake, and the market for oysters became so great that Baltimore merchants could not keep up with the demand.[83] Schooners and paddlewheel steamers were soon collecting oysters from new shucking houses that opened in waterfront villages encircling the bay. When the Civil War broke out, commercial shipping was halted for a time, but after the war the railroad came to the Eastern Shore. By 1866, the tracks had reached Crisfield.

The oystering boom completely transmogrified Crisfield's social and natural environment. It launched a new class of seafood elites into political prominence in the city, county, and state for nearly a hundred years. By the 1870s, Crisfield had surpassed Baltimore as the leading oyster port in the world, with six hundred oystering sail craft registered in the tiny port city. The yield culminated in 15 million bushels of oysters in 1880.[84] By 1884, twenty to thirty boxcars loaded with oysters left Crisfield each day for Wilmington, while countless more bushels were loaded on steamships for Baltimore.[85] The city had also become the major exporter of crabs in the United States.

By 1910, Crisfield had become the second most populous city in Maryland, with a population of over twelve thousand (four times its present population). More sailing vessels were registered there than at any other port in the United States.[86] Lawlessness came to Crisfield in the wake of the oystering boom. This formerly isolated, quiet Quaker and Methodist community became known far and wide for its casinos, saloons, bawdy houses, and unfettered violence. But "the fleshpots of Crisfield" were a minor intrusion compared with the invasion of the drudgers. They were captains of dredging vessels that descended from Baltimore, Cape Cod, and New Jersey by the hundreds to exploit the bay's providence, destroying the oyster beds as they came.

At the height of the boom, thousands of dredging boats plied the waters of the Chesapeake. Equipped with huge iron rakes for scraping oysters from the floor of the bay, each boat required a crew of eight men to wind its great hand-cranked winches.[87] Crews were enlisted from street corners, prisons, and poor houses. Some drudgers recruited penniless, uncomprehending immigrants straight off the ships that brought them to America.[88]

Evidently no crime was too heinous for this marauding element, for the worst drudgers shanghaied, enslaved, and then wantonly murdered their crews, "paying them off with the boom," as the saying went.[89] They plundered the Bay in defiance of all regulation, made war on honest watermen in Maryland and Virginia, and drove the "tongers" off the shallow bars that were theirs alone, by special license, to fish. Tongers were local watermen who worked alone in small ships from which they lifted oysters from the shallow bars with hand-operated tongs. This traditional method of oystering was not destructive of the fragile oyster beds, but the bay's ecological system has never recovered from the depredations of the drudgers.

So great was the lawlessness in the Chesapeake in that era that Maryland and Virginia were brought almost to the point of war.[90] In Virginia, "the drudgers assaulted the police, wrecked the towns, and raided the stores and saloons. The residents armed themselves, and formed a guard to keep the drudgers from coming ashore again. They were constantly at war with one another until the oysters in the Potomac River gave out, just as they had in the Tangier Sound."[91]

The Maryland legislature, after years of inaction because of the strength of the political influence wielded by the seafood packers, finally gave in to pressure from the tongers and created the celebrated Maryland Oyster Police. This attempt to bring law and order to the Chesapeake was largely futile, for, although the oyster police were reportedly valiant, their numbers were hopelessly inadequate in the face of the seven to ten thousand oyster boats working the bay.[92]

Contemporary observers placed the blame for the despoliation of the bay squarely on the packing plant owners who told "honest skippers" "to increase their catches or be replaced."[93]

> To make matters worse, the oyster packers and drudgers were making a lot of money, and their influence in the towns along the Bay was considerable. They contributed heavily to the support of political candidates, and openly bought votes on election day. They opposed any laws offered at the legislature that would strengthen the oyster police, and they attempted to place bureaucrats of their own choice in positions of authority.[94]

This reign of terror was finally brought to an end, by the collapse of the oyster industry in the 1920s. Soon afterward, "huge graveyards of rotting [ships] lay in the shallows around Crisfield."[95] The ravaged oyster beds were assailed by oyster diseases, which has all but destroyed them. In 1987 and 1988, the yield from the bay was 360,000 bushels, down from 15 million bushels in 1880 at the height of the boom.[96] The most severe declines in the oyster harvest have occurred in that reach of the bay that is worked by the industry in Somerset County.[97]

After the unprecedented cultural invasion brought on by the oystering boom had subsided, the natives of Crisfield gradually rebuilt their community, enacting prohibition laws and strict curfews to re-establish the earlier moral order. Isolationism and anti-materialism became more deeply ingrained in the local ethos. Civic elites and watermen alike had come to believe that outsiders represented a fundamentally different and menacing way of life.

Recent Development Pressures

What watermen fear is the set of capitalistic market forces that threaten to absorb and transform all other values, leaving the indigenous population once again embattled, belittled, cheated, displaced, and disinherited. Those who try to promote development in Crisfield and its environs encounter persistent opposition. Typically, the watermen oppose any project that threatens to introduce change or outsiders into their communities.

The experience of one developer, Clifton Justice, is prototypical. When in 1986 Justice tried to build a luxury townhouse development called "Pitchcroft" on eighty acres that he had acquired on Smith Island, the islanders became his relentless opponents. Justice had planned an airstrip for easier access to the island than the single existing ferryboat afforded, but the islanders objected that airplanes would collide with ospreys and herons and "buzz the houses," killing the waterfowl and disturbing the peace.

Justice had already agreed to what seemed to be generous concessions. All purchasers of the condominiums would be assessed several hundred dollars yearly toward a community fund that would pay for street lights and maintenance of the island's medical building. He promised a public swimming pool and other amenities. But the islanders' main concern, as it turned out, was not material in nature. They said there was a risk that "wealthier strangers would upset the cohesiveness of the community." [98]

At one public hearing, the islanders asked the developer what effects it would have on island children if those buying his vacation homes had children with newer toys and clothes: "Won't the Smith Island children feel ashamed of their simpler possessions and lifestyle?"[99] They launched a letter-writing campaign and expressed a concern that the "proposed development will undoubtedly introduce a new culture."[100] A local newspaper informally polled island residents about the proposed development and found that 60 percent strongly opposed it, 20 percent favored it, and 20 percent "didn't want to speak publicly against Mr. Justice or had no strong feelings."[101]

Justice was not easily daunted, however. First he conceded the airstrip, and then he abandoned his plans for a parking lot and agreed that no cars would be brought to the island. He persisted through hearings, law suits, and appeals over many more months. He gave up, however, when the islanders stonewalled on upgrading their water supply.

The sewage treatment plant had for some time failed to meet federal and state water quality standards, and construction on Pitchcroft could not begin until corrections were made. In 1989, after three years of haggling, Smith Islanders were still fending off a state mandate to replace their eight small, aging, contaminated, nonprofit, cooperative wells. The battle over the water supply con-

FIGURE 3.5 A Glimpse of Life on Smith Island

tinues as of this writing, but Mr. Justice has not been heard from for a long time.

Polanyi's words on the subject of cultural conquest seem extraordinarily prophetic when considered in the context of these struggles. Where cultural contact between people from different geographical regions occurs, he observed that:

the contact may have a devastating effect on the weaker part. Not economic exploitation as often assumed, but the disintegration of the cultural environment of the victim is then the cause of the degradation. The economic process may, naturally, supply the vehicle of the destruction, and almost invariably economic inferiority will make the weaker yield, but the immediate cause of his undoing is not for that economic reason. It lies in the lethal injury to the institutions in which his social existence is embodied. The result is loss of self respect and standards, whether the unit is a people or a class, whether the process springs from the so-called "culture conflict" or from the change in the position of a class within the confines of a society.[102]

The watermen of the Chesapeake seemed as cognizant as Polanyi was of the potentially destructive impacts of cultural invasion on the frail social fabric. Their antimaterialistic, communitarian ethos should not be unduly idealized. It was based on a realistic grasp of the social and material conditions required for subsistence and for maintenance of a unique way of life that they value immensely. Within the limits defined by the local culture, watermen are as attentive to their individual interests as anyone else. Their view of their interests, however, is unlike that of neoclassical economists. A waterman might rank his independent way of life "on the water" second only to survival in his preference ordering. Any number of other values, such as family, church, and community, might come before wealth in a waterman's utility function.

THE ECONOMIC DEVELOPMENT COMMISSION OF SOMERSET COUNTY

This chapter has shown how historical factors that stem from the county's earliest settlements became woven together to create institutions and cultures that mediated strongly against social change. Whether landholding planters in the north or seafood packers in the south, the dominant group in each of Somerset's main sectors sustained its own interests by thwarting development that threatened to import higher wages, worker benefits, and genuine opportunities for the poor. Considering the longstanding political dominance of these economic elites and the resistance to change that many common people manifested also, how can we explain the development efforts that occurred in Somerset during the 1980s?

From the Great Depression onward, the economic conditions that historically had supported the planters' regime had been eroding. The diminishing fortunes of the growers can be attributed to several causes. Farm labor shortages had been a serious problem since the great outmigration of blacks in the thirties and forties. From then on, planters relied increasingly on migrant labor, which carried its own set of problems.[103] The national civil rights movement put an end to Jim Crow laws and other instruments of racial oppression, further eroding a longstanding source of advantage.

Decades of worldwide overproduction of vegetables and grain had further devastated the agricultural sector.[104] In the 1980s, the Reagan administration's retrenchment policy, called "new federalism," placed new burdens on state and local governments nationwide, forcing them to search for new ways to raise revenues, and the Eastern Shore's local governments were not immune to these harsh impacts of federal policy.[105] Economic decline continued thus to worsen in Somerset County, and, in 1981, government and business leaders jointly established the Economic Development Commission (EDC) in response to these combined pressures. The EDC was structured as a quasi-public, policymaking body whose members included representatives both from the public and from the private sectors of the county and its two towns.[106] Its mission was to build local support for economic development and attract jobs and capital to the county.

There seemed to be almost a full consensus among county residents that it would be good if economic decline could be arrested and more opportunities provided for the county's young people, but many of the individuals that interviewed for this study were passively sitting on the EDC's growth task forces while privately confessing that they hoped growth never came. There was a striking ambivalence that surfaced in the course of this research: a discrepancy between words and deeds.[107] This ambivalence becomes easier to understand when we consider that vague statements of grand purpose are useful for those who are interested in garnering votes or building a following, but following through distributes costs and makes political enemies. In these small communities, few people were willing to make enemies of their neighbors or the county's ruling elites, who were divided on the growth issue. Still, there were some individuals who tried earnestly to bring industry to Somerset County.

EDC officials claimed that the county could not afford to be selective about the kinds of industries that it tried to attract, and the results of their efforts reflect that desperation. By the time this research ended, they had succeeded in recruiting and retaining little more than a medium-security state prison just outside of Princess Anne. Negotiations for this project were conducted with state officials in secret, and it was not until the ground was broken that it became general knowledge that a prison was being built.

The Eastern Correctional Institution has provided a few jobs for the local people, but it has cost the county and state hundreds of thousands of dollars in compensatory payments to residents whose wells went dry the day that it opened, and the housing boom that EDC officials expected the prison to stimulate never occurred. Furthermore, because the state's starting salary for correctional officers at the prison was approximately double that of the members of Princess Anne's police force, the town was forced immediately to double the base salaries of its policemen, lest it lose them all to the prison. When the next election came, the county officials who had supported the prison project were turned out of office. EDC officials were not deterred by these setbacks, however, and they continued to try to entice mobile capital into Somerset County. The case studies that follow address the issue of economic development in the two towns.

4

PRINCESS ANNE, 1986–1991

The previous chapter explained how an oligarchy became established in Somerset County in colonial times and maintained its power well into the twentieth century, in spite of a series of potentially restructuring events. This chapter gives an account of instigating events that occurred in Princess Anne in the recent era and reports how the governing group responded to those threats.

For three centuries, until 1990, county courthouse elites had dominated the town government, and no black had ever been elected to public office in Princess Anne. Then, the 1990 elections provided a severe jolt, for the voters chose a woman, a black, a retired research biochemist from New Jersey, and a music teacher from New York City to fill four out of five seats on the town commission. The electoral uprising represented an apparent restructuring of the regime, but this chapter will show that the "revolt" was soon got in hand. Still, change was in process, and restructuring efforts had been ongoing in the black community for several years. Another instigating event was the serious decline in agriculture, because it undermined the economic foundation of the planters' regime. Hence the development policy that Princess Anne adopted in the 1980s should be understood as the response of governing elites to another one of a long series of threats to their economic and political dominance.

FIGURE 4.1 Somerset County Courthouse in Princess Anne

ECONOMIC PRESSURES

In Princess Anne, where the people were faced with a steady exodus of businesses, rising unemployment, and strain on the town coffers, the governing group had long acceded to the idea that growth was needed, but, until 1986, little action had been taken to bring it about. Elites were slow to embrace a program of thoroughgoing economic development, because they feared the kinds of changes that growth might bring.[1] In this community that had always been sustained by low-wage, labor-intensive industries, the lesson of the state prison was not lost on the governing group. That is, some elites worried that an influx of new business concerns would compete for the supply of cheap labor by introducing benefits and higher wages. Because this group's interest had been in maintaining low wages, low taxes, and a large, dependent, seasonal labor force, a high unemployment rate was to their economic advantage.[2] There were concerns too about what effects growth might have on the social fabric, the social structure, and the racial caste system to which the dominant group seemed largely committed.[3]

FIGURE 4.2 Courthouse Officials

But by the 1980s, the decline in agriculture was far advanced, and all that was left of Princess Anne's once aristocratic ruling group was a much reduced remnant that is perhaps best described by its name in the local idiom: "the good-ole-boy machine." Since farming had ceased to be a viable option for the younger generation of many landholding families, some members of this group were becoming ready to reallocate their economic and political resources. A number of such families, whose estates bordered the town, had come to believe that their prospective fortunes now lay in commercial land-use development. They had supported the establishment of the Economic Development Commission of Somerset County (EDC) in 1981, no doubt also believing that growth would be conducive to the general good. Princess Anne thus clung to caretaker government until a series of events occurred in the 1980s that pointed toward a modification of the regime.

THE BLACK COMMUNITY'S CHALLENGE

A legal challenge came in 1985, when a black citizen named James Mullen brought a class action voting rights suit against the town, charging that the at-large voting system was discriminatory. State Attorney General Sachs advised that the town was legally vulnerable, and the commissioners agreed to settle the case out of court. Two districts, one of them predominantly black, were then created to replace the at-large system. Of the three town commissioners, two would represent specific districts, and one would remain at-large.

James Mullen was represented, in this case, by Christopher Brown, a civil rights lawyer from Baltimore, who defined two other goals for the black community: ending the requirement for separate voter registration for state and municipal elections and annexation of Greenwood, a predominantly black neighborhood. Brown and others believed that these changes would augment the electoral power of African Americans and gain better services for the residents of Greenwood than the county provided.

Although the demand for voting districts was immediately successful, that was not the case for the other two goals. In 1986, Mullen and others petitioned the town commissioners to annex Greenwood, but the town attorney ruled that the number of signatures on the petition was too few and the proposed boundaries too vague.[4] Dual voter registration remained in force until universal registration was implemented statewide in 1990.

Encouraged nevertheless by the creation of a predominantly black voting district, James Mullen filed as a candidate for the Princess Anne Town Commission in District 2 in June 1986. The incumbent was Roland Collins, president of the town commission, who was seeking a third term. Collins represented the traditional courthouse elites. He was a native of the lower shore, and his wife was from Princess Anne. He had retired from a successful business in nearby Salisbury. Collins won the election by a margin of fifty to twenty-nine votes, indicating how small the voter turnout was, especially among blacks.[5]

To summarize, a legal challenge to the regime was mounted by activists in the black community in 1985, resulting in the creation of two voting districts, one of which was predominantly black. But, without the annexation of Greenwood or other changes, this did not result in the election of a black candidate in 1986. In 1988, the town elections were *pro forma:* there were no challengers. The introduction of electoral districts was not enough to bring about a restructuring of the regime.

THE GROWTH MACHINE

At about the same time that Roland Collins was elected to his third term as president of the town commission, he was also elected to serve as president of the Economic Development Commission of Somerset County (EDC), and he made few distinctions between these two roles. As the *de facto* mayor, his foremost concern was to pursue economic development for the town, and he was loath to recognize the legitimacy of any dissenting opinion or alternative policy proposals. In this manner, economic development was placed at the top of the town commission's agenda.

In the fall of the same year, a real estate broker named Harvey Hastings moved into the county and opened a realty firm in Princess Anne. He soon emerged as the mastermind behind a new growth coalition that was composed of private business interests, real estate interests, and public officials. Hastings came to Princess Anne with the drive and know-how to weave these elements into a tight knit partnership and to get things done. In December, he organized the Princess Anne Chamber of Commerce, which brought the coalition partners together in one body and supplied them with organizational resources and a recognized public role. Over the next three years, this coalition expanded its influence as it also advanced its proposals for tax and land-use changes that purported to foster economic growth and prosperity for the town. Whether in fact it accomplished these aims was later hotly disputed.

A third event occurred two years later, when the town commissioners employed a former prison warden to replace the departing town manager. Upon assuming his new duties, Wayne Winebrenner also went to work as an agent of Harvey Hastings' realty firm. Mayor Roland Collins owned land just outside the town that he became interested in developing during this period. It is possible that he was influenced by Hastings, who was himself developing a nearby tract called "Fairwinds." Commissioner Keith Miller was likewise developing land on the outskirts of town. Thus by the summer of 1989, the town manager and two of the three town commissioners had become what Logan and Molotch call modern "rentiers," "the people directly involved in the exchange of places and collection of rents," who seek to profit from land-use intensification.[6]

Finally, in the fall of 1989, Collins and Miller appointed Carol Wink to serve out the term of the third commissioner, Royce Windsor, who had moved out of town. The appointment provoked criticism among the townspeople, because Wink was the wife of a prominent developer, Gary Wink, and the manager of twenty rental properties, but was not a registered voter until just before being sworn into office.[7] With all three town commissioners and the town manager involved in land speculation, rentals, sales, or development, and with the mayor serving as president of the EDC, a shift from caretaker government had clearly occurred. Hastings, the broker, by providing the leadership and the material incentives to go along—in the form of commissions, rents, and profits, or promises thereof—had reshaped the town government into a growth machine.

GROWTH POLICY AND DEVELOPING OPPOSITION

When Roland Collins ran for his third term as town commissioner of Princess Anne in 1986, he embraced a platform for growth. In office, he energetically executed his campaign promises to increase the town's tax base by annexation, bring in industry and jobs, and provide loans for downtown businesses.[8] No opposition to this program surfaced, and in 1988 all three candidates for the commission ran unopposed. But by 1990, electoral support for Collins and his cohorts had vanished, and no fewer than eight challengers campaigned for seats on the town commission. Policies that initially were acceptable to the townspeople had, within four years, become abhorrent. What had happened?

"Increase the Town's Tax Base by Annexation"

After the 1986 elections, the African American candidates who had unsuccessfully run for office in the town and county created an organization to advance the goals of the black community, especially the annexation of Greenwood. The town commissioners supported the proposed annexation and worked with the new organization's leader, Kirkland Hall, to gain the required signatures for the annexation petition. Mayor Collins argued that this would add needed revenues to the town's tax base and would extend municipal services to the residents of Greenwood. Collins thus framed the proposed annexation as a developmental policy that would benefit the town and redress longstanding allocational inequities suffered by blacks. Commissioner Keith Miller also favored the plan, but since he was not known for his sympathies with the black community, there was speculation that his ownership of real property in Greenwood had shaped his view.

Despite outspoken support from Collins and Miller, the annexation effort bogged down in controversy and ultimately foundered because of an unexpected source of opposition. Leon Johnson, a black leader in Princess Anne, and Craig Webster, a white civic leader from Deal Island, were the chief officers of the Somerset County Civic Association that owned the Greenwood Garden Apartments. Because it was the largest nonprofit, HUD-subsidized housing project in Greenwood, their signatures were required if the annexation petition was to succeed.

Johnson and Webster opposed the annexation of the apartment project. They argued that the imposition of additional taxes would outweigh the benefit of the few services that would be added to those already provided by the management. Webster further believed that annexation would lead to gentrification and other land-use changes that eventually would drive out most of Greenwood's black residents and mainly benefit landlords such as Keith Miller and the developers to whom he had sold real property in the neighborhood. Webster pointed out that, unlike the county, the town had a "livability code" for rental property; thus if Greenwood should become part of Princess Anne, much of the neighborhood's low-cost housing would become subject to condemnation. He argued that land-use improvements that would raise the value of the properties and hence the town's assessable base would also raise property taxes beyond the affordability of Greenwood's working-class black homeowners.

Disputes over the annexation of Greenwood dragged on for more than three years, causing rancorous divisions in the black community and frustrating the town commissioners. About 30 percent of the neighborhood's residents ultimately withdrew their signatures from the annexation petition. Others remained convinced that by pursuing the annexation that had been advocated by Christopher Brown, the civil rights attorney, the town commissioners were acting in the interest of the black community.

Other annexation efforts were more successful. In 1987, the town annexed a 185-acre mobile home park that had recently been erected on farmland that Commissioner Keith Miller had sold to a developer. The town also annexed a housing development and another large tract belonging to the developer Gary Wink.

FIGURE 4.3 The Washington Hotel in Downtown Princess Anne:
A Gathering Place for Elites

A controversy erupted the following year, when Keith Miller petitioned the county zoning board to allow him to place a 140-unit trailer park next to the two-hundred-year-old Glebe House that had recently been restored.[9] Historical preservation groups were up in arms, and others argued that the scenic approach to Princess Anne would be spoiled by another large trailer park. County zoning officials heard objections from more than twenty people, including Robert Erickson, the chairman of the Princess Anne zoning board.[10] But Keith Miller, purporting to testify for the town of Princess Anne in his capacity as a town commissioner, asserted that since the proposed trailer park was within one mile of Princess Anne, the town had a right to offer an opinion—"and the town has no objection."[11] This statement did not sit well with opponents, for Miller was the owner of the property in question as well as being a town commissioner.[12] The incident appeared to be politically inconsequential, however, because a few days later Miller was re-elected to the Princess Anne Town Commission and the county approved his trailer park.

Zoning conflicts resurfaced in 1989, when Harvey Hastings, the real estate broker, petitioned the Princess Anne zoning board to allow him to place trailers in his forty-six acre subdivision called Fairwinds, which was in the process of being annexed by the town. In the hearings that followed, Robert Erickson, the town zoning board chairman, recommended against it.[13] The ramifications of Erickson's decision were to be far-reaching, but the issue was eclipsed by a matter of greater immediacy.

"Bring Industry and Jobs to Princess Anne"

No one had objected when Mayor Collins announced his intention to recruit jobs and industry for the town, but most of the people were taken unawares when in June 1989 Shellfish Inc. suddenly opened a clam processing plant in the center of historic Princess Anne.[14] Preparations for the plant opening had proceeded with little public notice or comment following two years of secret negotiations with the EDC.[15] To many citizens, however, the recruitment of an industrial processing plant was in complete violation of the downtown revitalization plan that had just been unveiled by Maryland planners, calling for the town to "focus on its historic assets, attract more tourists, improve housing, plan for the growth of government office space, and utilize the potential of UMES."[16]

Moreover, there was another objection that quickly took on greater urgency. Within days of the plant's opening, Princess Anne was enveloped by a stench so foul that children and the elderly were getting sick and were forced to stay indoors.[17] A letter to the local newspaper blamed public officials, saying that the town commissioners, the EDC, and the county commissioners should "hang their heads in shame" for letting "a stinking project like this" be perpetrated on the town without having investigated what kinds of impacts it would have on the community.[18]

Mayor Collins explained that the noxious effluvium was emanating from holding tanks where wastewater was being stored on the premises of the clam plant, the local sewer system being inadequate to handle the large volume being produced. Equipment had been ordered that would solve the problem within three to six weeks, he assured the distraught citizens. It emerged within days, however, that the problem was not limited to the wastewater holding tanks, for sickening gasses had begun seeping through the sewers into the public library and other buildings, now forcing people outdoors.[19] At the town meeting in September, citizens presented a petition demanding that the commissioners do something about the clam plant's stench. Two weeks later, a letter to the editor announced the organization of a grass-roots protest movement called People United (P.U.!).

> JUST SAY NO!
> We are now united . . . People United . . . call us P.U. We will not stop working to save our town until the last putrid clam smell is only an olfactory memory. . . . "Just Say No" to the desecration of our air. JUST SAY NO to elected and appointed officials who permit the clam plant to discharge waste water that does not pass sanitary code requirements. . . . JUST SAY NO to the "quick fix" to unemployment. . . . Say no to reckless progress, but please *say yes* to controlled growth that benefits all. . . . SAY YES TO P.U.—we meet tonight . . . in the Princess Anne library.
>
> Ritchie C. Shoemaker, M.D.[20]

In October, the town commissioners adopted an odor ordinance in response to continuing pressure, but P.U.'s largely white, middle-class membership was not mollified, and its spokesman appealed to the county sanitary commission to exercise its authority. But Tony Bruce, the sanitary commission's attorney, informed Dr. Shoemaker that to impose restrictions on the clam plant would be an overextension of power, in his view. Rebuffed by the sanitary commission, Shoemaker continued to appeal to various authorities.

Some people in the town believed that Tony Bruce was a central figure in what was locally called "the good ole boy machine." Between 1985 and 1990, Bruce served at one time or another as attorney to the sanitary commission, secretary of the EDC, attorney for the county health department (that was responsible for establishing whether violations of the odor ordinance had occurred), and attorney for Underwood and Hall (the development firm that worked for both Harvey Hastings and Roland Collins on their respective land development schemes). He was also solicitor for the city of Crisfield, a trustee of the University of Maryland Eastern Shore, chairman of the board of the Regional Development Center at UMES, and chairman of the Princess Anne Downtown Improvement Association.

Bruce had longstanding personal and professional connections with Danny Long, the local delegate to the Maryland General Assembly and chairman (as his father had been) of the House Judiciary Committee. When Long resigned his seat in order to replace his uncle as the local circuit court judge, Bruce was appointed to serve for the remainder of Long's term in the General Assembly. Bruce was also a member of the Peninsula Bank's Advisory Board for Somerset County. (Danny Long and Commissioner Keith Miller's father also served on the bank's Board of Directors.)

This partial list of Bruce's affiliations illustrates the interlocking associational and status networks that often remained intact through generations in this community and were characteristic of its social and political structure. It illustrates the phenomenon that historians have referred to as "courthouse gangs."[21] It shows what Shoemaker and P.U. were up against in opposing the good ole boy machine.

Renewed Conflict over Annexation and Zoning

When in July 1989 the Princess Anne zoning board chairman, Robert Erickson, recommended against allowing Harvey Hastings to place trailers on sixteen acres in Fairwinds, the town commissioners refused to accept the appointed board's recommendation and ordered Erickson to reconsider his decision.[22] But after reconsideration, Erickson saw no reason to change his mind. The town commissioners then rezoned and annexed the land anyway, overruling the board.[23] Not long afterward, Robert Erickson was dismissed. "A man cannot serve two masters," Mayor Collins intoned, explaining that he had fired the zoning board chairman for conflict of interest because he was active in P.U.![24]

This act so angered residents of Princess Anne that several people considered running for office. The conflict-of-interest charge that was leveled at Erickson impressed them as especially hypocritical in view of Collins's position as chairman of the EDC and its role

in harboring the foul clam plant.[25] When Collins subsequently petitioned the zoning board to approve a zoning change for his own
property under conditions that were similar to the controversial
Fairwinds case, Robert Erickson decided to run as a candidate for the
town commission.[26] Former Commissioner Royce Windsor (who
had moved back into town) also declared his candidacy at that time.
"There's a lot more in Princess Anne that stinks than just the clam
plant," observed Dr. Shoemaker.[27]

"Provide Loans for Downtown Businesses"

At the town meeting in January, residents complained about continuing odors indoors and out. One person said that bad smells were
"permeating all over the house," another had contacted an extermi-
nator, and a third complained that her husband was sick from nau-
seating gasses that were seeping into their home.[28] The town
commissioners responded that they had applied to the state for a
$1.7 million industrial development loan for Shellfish to enable it to
improve wastewater management at the plant, but residents were
not appeased. A letter to the local newspaper protested:

> The Town Commissioners may feel that such a loan is consis-
> tent with plans for development in Princess Anne. I don't. I
> think this enterprise will do more to ruin business and prop-
> erty values . . . while substantially diminishing the quality of
> life for the majority of the town's residents. . . . How can a
> small town that currently takes pride in its historic homes,
> County courthouse, and university, possibly develop any of
> those assets if it stinks? . . . local support . . . is limited and
> opposition is significant.[29]

Opposition increased after a citizen, Robert Hooks, while
clearing away underbrush at his home, discovered clam juice flow-
ing in a ditch that empties into the Manokin River. "This definitely
was an isolated incident," a Shellfish official protested, and dirt barriers were constructed around the perimeter of the plant to prevent
wastewater from escaping again.[30] But one week later, the Maryland
Department of the Environment cited the plant for another run-off
incident in the same ditch. Dr. Shoemaker then wrote to Governor
Schaefer:

I can tell you about the recent spills of clam plant wash water full of brine, boiler blowdowns, and dumping of wastewater into a tributary of the Manokin River. . . . The main issue initially was 80 new jobs versus quality of life. . . . Now, however, the 80 sweatshop minimum wage jobs are taking an allocation of 50,000 gallons a day from our . . . sewer plant. . . . How many jobs will we lose in this decade by maintaining 80 jobs in an environmentally insensitive industry? Is this the classic example of a quick fix? . . . Clearly our local officials have decided to support the clam plant without regard to its adverse affects on our community. The clam smells are jeopardizing our Town development, and the waste water is overtaxing the capacity of our sewer plant. We are suffering a far greater loss than just retardation of our revitalization, reduction in tourist revenues, loss of property values and elimination of free enjoyment of living and working in this small town. . . . We will soon be in a crisis of sewer allocation. . . . We couldn't stop the smells. We want you to try.[31]

There was an acrimonious public hearing in March, in which P.U. asked the town commissioners to withdraw their support for the loan to Shellfish and pleaded for citizen input into future land-use decisions such as what industries would be permitted to locate in Princess Anne.

Mayor Collins berated the witnesses, bellowing "You talk about 'citizen input.' Hah! If you want 'citizen input' then you don't need elected officials!"[32]

Robert Hooks shouted back in reply: "Talkin' to you is like *talkin' to the mule! Talkin' to the mule!*"[33] Hooks had earlier written to the local newspaper, saying, "I like living here in this one horse town, but there's a mule that's trying to run it."[34]

Alleged stubbornness notwithstanding, the commissioners voted unanimously to scuttle the loan. They confessed that they had received erroneous information about the degree of liability the town could incur. Meanwhile, it had come to light that an officer of Shellfish had recently been indicted in New Jersey for being involved in an international drug ring.[35] The clam plant closed the day of the hearing.

Despite Tony Bruce's earlier disclaimer of its authority, the sanitary commission ordered the plant to stop releasing wastewater into the sewer. The closing of the plant and the commissioners' decision to withdraw support for the state loan were disappointing to the management of Shellfish and its eighty or so full- and part-time workers. They too wrote letters to the newspaper and came before the commissioners to ask for consideration of their plight.

It is hard to specify why support for the clam plant collapsed on every front, but a moratorium on sewer allocations seems to have been the *coup de grace*. The Maryland Department of the Environment (MDE) advised Harvey Hastings that the Fairwinds subdivision would not be permitted to proceed until it could obtain a sewer allocation, but none could be granted so long as the clam plant was in operation. The Princess Anne sewer plant was already operating in excess of its design capacity.[36] With all new land development thus brought to a standstill, Tony Bruce, who was secretary of the EDC and attorney for both Fairwinds and for Mayor Collins' planned housing project, apparently had concluded that imposing restrictions on the clam plant was within the sanitary commission's legal purview after all.

Shellfish closed the clam plant owing the sanitary commission seventy thousand dollars and leaving Princess Anne with an unpaid corporate tax bill of twenty thousand dollars. In addition, according to the plant manager, there were seventy five thousand gallons of sludge and ninety thousand gallons of wastewater stored on the property and "now undergoing anaerobic digestion which causes odors, especially on hot days."[37]

In April, Shirley Richards filed as an at-large candidate to run against Roland Collins in the June elections. A native of Princess Anne and the recognized local historian, she was also the recording secretary for P.U.

More Industry and Jobs for Princess Anne

Even though the sludge and wastewater stored at the clam plant continued to befoul the air in Princess Anne, many residents looked forward to a better civic atmosphere. The ordeal that had so long agitated the community seemed nearly to be over. But in May, some townspeople learned that a medical waste storage and transfer company was negotiating with town officials about relocating its facility in Princess Anne.

"Anything from body parts and fluids to rubber gloves and syringes" would be stored in a large warehouse on a small lot in town, said the owner at a special public hearing. He projected that, in five years, the family-run business might employ up to ten people. He had been asked by a former schoolmate, Harvey Hastings, to consider locating in Princess Anne.[38]

Many of the citizens who attended the hearing seemed to feel that a facility of that sort would be as bad for the town as the clam plant had been. For some, this development was the last straw. Attempting to placate townspeople who were boiling with anger, the commissioners promised another hearing before a final decision. There never was another hearing on the matter, however, because an entirely new town commission was elected six weeks later in an unprecedented electoral uprising.

How It Happened

The voting rights lawsuit, the redistricting that resulted, and the attempts to annex the sizable black neighborhood of Greenwood had apparently stirred racial fears among some of Princess Anne's residents, for early in 1988, a prominent member of the local business establishment proposed a set of changes to the town charter, arguing that local government would be improved if ways could be found to "bring in new blood." This could be accomplished, he suggested, by enlarging the pool of those qualified to run for public office by including nonresident owners of businesses in Princess Anne. Note that they were already allowed to vote in the town elections.

A charter review committee made recommendations to the town commissioners, which they, in turn, submitted to the public in referendum. The following reforms were adopted to begin with the 1990 election: The number of commissioners was increased from three to five, with two commissioners representing each of the two districts and one remaining at-large; the term of office was expanded from two years to four years; and the terms were staggered. The proposal that business owners residing outside of the town limits should be qualified to run for public office was defeated. The revisions to the town charter that were initiated by conservative members of the white business establishment in response to the threat of increased black voting had the unintended consequence of strengthening insurgents. These changes created important preconditions for the upset election.

THE 1990 ELECTION

When "Meet the Candidates Night," which I attended, was held one week before the municipal elections, the two incumbents who sought re-election, Roland Collins and Keith Miller, declined to attend. Of the eight challengers, all except Bill Rice and Shirley Richards attended the forum and expressed their views about governing the town. The participating candidates were as follows:

Robert Erickson: Retired biochemist from New Jersey and ousted Princess Anne Zoning Board chairman.
Manford Frank: Local teacher and agent of Harvey Hasting, the real estate broker.
Garland Hayward: Teacher and high school athletics director—an African American.[39]
Charles Nittel: Bed and breakfast owner from New Jersey.
Vernon Tompkins: Retired music teacher from New York City.
Royce Windsor: Local hardware store manager and former town commissioner.

The candidates aired four complaints against the incumbent commissioners: (1) There is widespread conflict of interest in the town government; (2) decisions are made behind closed doors; (3) the incumbents are not responsive to the views of the people; and (4) the town has come under the control of real estate interests. Only Manford Frank took exception to the thrust of these remarks, understandably, for he was an agent of Hastings's realty firm.

Garland Hayward, the black candidate, said that he would like to encourage blacks to participate in town government, and Vernon Tompkins voiced his support of that goal.[40] Tompkins later visited Hayward at home, and, after exchanging views, the two men decided to run as ticketmates in District 2. They posted campaign signs in the neighborhood pairing their names. On June 26, 1990, 37 percent of the eligible voters in Princess Anne cast their ballots as follows:

District I		District II	
Frank	81	Hayward	57
Erickson	75	Tompkins	43
Rice	69	Wink	37
Nittel	68	Windsor	34

At-Large			
Richards	153	Collins	78

Shirley Richards received the largest number of votes, but she declined to serve as president of the town commission. The new commissioners then elected Vernon Tompkins, a seven-year resident of Princess Anne, to serve as the de facto mayor. Tompkins explained to me his decision to run for office: "I wasn't down here to change their town; I moved here because I liked it the way it was. But things were done to people who objected to the clam plant at a public meeting, and I couldn't live here and see this going on around me—people being intimidated, threats being made—and do nothing. It became a moral thing." [41]

THE AFTERMATH

The jubilation of the insurgents was premature. Ordinarily, a mere handful of people attended the town meetings, but now crowds of as many as seventy turned out to bait and heckle the new officeholders. This unruly throng was not constituted of people who ordinarily attended town meetings or voted in local elections. Possibly it was the novelty of seeing a black American in public office that prompted them to come to the meetings and jeer. Or perhaps their disruptive presence was engineered by more prominent citizens, as some people believe. There was, after all, a history of racially motivated rabble-rousing and mob violence in the town. But regardless of who or what drew this rough element, their foot-stomping, racial taunts, and shouted interruptions prevented the officials from following their agenda or focusing on the town's business.

By September, the disorders had escalated to shoving and threatened fisticuffs, and Craig Webster was so concerned about the potential for violence that he invited two television stations to be present as a means of social control.[42] In October, TV cameras were running and the meeting was orderly. By then, Tompkins had resigned from the town commission.

Within less than six months, the "good ole boy machine" had partially reversed the outcome of the election and re-established its former control of the town. Vernon Tompkins was hounded from office. He was an unnamed target, it seemed, of a newspaper column entitled "Somerset City" that was written by Harvey Hastings and published weekly in the *Somerset Herald*. This column, first appearing two weeks after the election, was billed as "humor and commentary," but many readers were neither amused nor enlightened. The articles were replete with demeaning racial stereotypes that seemed to be aimed at Hayward and thinly veiled references to Tompkins as "King Harold," an effeminate character depicted as carrying lace hankies, frequenting "the Satanical Gardens," and residing at "the corner of Sodom and Gomorrah."[43] Tompkins, who suffered from multiple sclerosis, experienced an exacerbation of symptoms as a result of increased stress, and, after serving fewer than ninety days in office, was forced to step down.

FIGURE 4.4 Princess Anne Town Meeting

Hastings immediately discontinued his journalistic sorties, and the timing seemed to confirm the sentiment in the town that he and Richard Crumbacker, the newspaper editor, had accomplished their mission. Shortly afterward, Shirley Richards admonished Crumbacker: "If you can do this to Vernon, then as soon as I take a position you don't like, you can do it to me. Vernon was chosen by the people of Princess Anne in a free election, just as I was. But once we stand by and permit this to be done to even one person, we've eliminated the democratic process and we don't need elections!"[44]

Shirley Richards succeeded Vernon Tompkins as mayor, but, within seven days of assuming the office, apparently intimidated by the menacing political climate and a rash of anonymous threats, she also stepped down. Robert Erickson then became the third person to serve as mayor, and Richards continued to serve as a town commissioner.[45] A special election was held to fill the District 2 vacancy that Tompkins' resignation had created, and perhaps it is indicative of the racial climate in the community that not one African American stepped forward as a candidate in the predominantly black voting district that James Mullen had gone to court to fight for five years earlier. Thus Carol Wink, after defeating another white woman candidate by thirty-eight to twenty-five votes in November, was reinstated in the position from which the electorate had removed her in June.

Only weeks after the June upset election, some people in the community learned that the town manager, Wayne Winebrenner, had approached Garland Hayward with informal offers to have a basketball court built in one of Princess Anne's black neighborhoods. When Hayward later declined to support ticket-mate Vernon Tompkins in his effort to dismiss Winebrenner, this signified to many people that the town's first black commissioner had been co-opted. With Hastings' agent, Manny Frank, already on board and Hayward seemingly brought to heel, the replacement of Vernon Tompkins by former Commissioner Wink reduced the number of reliable reformers on the commission to two. The town manager retained his position, and Roland Collins continued his efforts to manipulate land use in Princess Anne from his new position as head of the recently established Rural Development Center at UMES.

DISCUSSION

In keeping with the embeddedness argument advanced by Granovetter and other scholars, it has been observed that "the character of local politics depends greatly on the nature of a community's associational life."[46] One can see that the associational features of Princess Anne did not produce an environment in which democracy could easily gain a foothold. In June 1990, the electorate briefly held the town commissioners accountable for their unpopular economic development policies, but democratic norms were weak and there were no autonomous institutions capable of enforcing them. Nor were there independent bases of opposition to the good ole boy machine.

The governing group's interlocking associations and networks extended beyond Princess Anne, reaching into county and state institutions as well. Thus, when Roland Collins failed to achieve re-election to the Princess Anne Town Commission, he established a new institutional base for himself at UMES, from which he continued pressing the levers of power. Political parties provide opposition in some local jurisdictions, but their activities were virtually insignificant at the level of small local governments on Maryland's Eastern Shore. Even the one newspaper served as an organ of the governing group.

Given that Garland Hayward was the first African American ever to be elected in Princess Anne, one might have expected black political organizations to rally to the support of the new commissioners, but unambiguous endorsements from that quarter were not forthcoming. Instead, the black leader, Kirkland Hall, wrote a letter to the local newspaper in which he expressed reservations about whether the new commissioners were qualified for public office

and, at the same time, urged the townspeople to give them a chance.[47] There was widespread criticism within the black community of some of their leaders, who were seen as forming a particular kind of alliance with established power. They were sometimes referred to as "system blacks," meaning that they made accommodation with the ruling group. The co-optation of black leaders is an established pattern in black belt counties in the Deep South, and Somerset conformed to the type.[48] "The trouble with the black community organizations," said one informant, "is that the leaders have one foot in both camps." But Kirkland Hall was no system black,

FIGURE 4.5
Kirkland Hall, a Civic Leader

as his subsequent actions made clear. Hence his letter should probably be interpreted as a diplomatic attempt to assuage white hostility against the new commissioners.

I am convinced that these complex relationships cannot be understood outside of the context of the local culture. Elites had a fine-tuned sensitivity to the political climate in the black community, and they carefully crafted their framing of issues accordingly. The paternalistic understandings that blacks and whites shared in this isolated community provided the governing group with a means of influencing the black people that outsiders lacked.[49] The local people of both races were, after all, rooted together in a place bounded by mores and tradition. Generation after generation, they had been locked in an ongoing dialogue with each other—a dialogue that was informed by a common heritage of institutions, customs, and values. All were participants in a way of life that they shared for better or worse: a common culture. It is not surprising, then, that Roland Collins and Tony Bruce had some strong supporters in the African American community. It is also understandable that, because the disinterested egalitarianism of many outsiders such as Tomkins and Erickson was foreign to the local experience, it did not register in the black community as offering the possibility of a potentially empowering alliance.

Princess Anne is very small, and the pool of citizens who might serve on its various governing boards and committees is small. Hence retirees like Erickson and Tomkins were sometimes recruited because they had the time, interest, and ability to perform these civic duties. But because they were financially independent outsiders who were not imbued with the local culture and mindset, they were also a potential source of opposition to the regime. Erickson demonstrated this when he served as chairman of the Princess Anne Planning and Zoning Board. It appeared, at the time of this study, that if an alliance between this element and the black political organization should ever come into being, a potent challenge to the regime could perhaps be mounted. Later events show that this is in fact what occurred.

TWO YEARS LATER

More than two years have elapsed since these events happened, and, as of this writing, the restructuring of Princess Anne's regime appears to be a fait accompli. In 1993, the American Civil Liberties Union (ACLU), cooperating with the local NAACP's new president, Kirkland Hall, filed a lawsuit against Princess Anne. The plaintiff alleged that the local practice of extending the franchise to nonresident property owners diluted the votes of black citizens and thus violated the 1965 Voting Rights Act.

Princess Anne's first black commissioner, Garland Hayward, who had by then become the de facto mayor, initially joined with commissioners Manford Frank and Carol Wink in asserting that to prevent nonresident property owners from voting was the same thing as "taxation without representation." He announced that the town would fight the lawsuit to the bitter end. But afterward, harkening to the uproar that this created in the black community, Hayward reconsidered. At a later town meeting, he made a courageous and stirring speech in which he explained his change of heart and then used his swing vote to enable the town to settle the lawsuit and revise its charter. Thus ended the town's archaic and arguably unconstitutional property qualification for voting, which had been an important source of the courthouse elite's inordinate political influence in the town relative to the black majority.

I have been told that Tony Bruce, Roland Collins, and Harvey Hastings were not amused. Bruce circulated a petition to bring to referendum a proposal to disincorporate Princess Anne. He reports that he has enough signatures, and the ACLU is monitoring this development.[50] It appears unlikely that a referendum to disincorporate could succeed, however, since the NAACP, under Kirkland Hall's leadership, is organizing a voter registration drive among the town's black majority.

Carol Wink resigned, explaining that she planned to move out of town, and Garland Hayward had no difficulty pursuading the other commissioners that it was fitting to appoint an African American from District 2 to complete Wink's term of office. Thus, of the original good ole boy faction, only Manford Frank remains as a member of Princess Anne's governing body. The rest of the town commission is constituted of a white woman, two blacks, and a research biochemist from New Jersey. Vernon Tompkins presently serves as an unofficial ombudsman to the town government, attending town meetings, dispatching letters to the editor, posting notices around town that instruct the residents and lawmakers as to the rights and responsibilities of self-government, and, in general, keeping it honest.

Conclusion

Princess Anne's culture and social structure nourished a long-standing oligarchy that discouraged—one might even say crushed—competition.[51] Cultural taboos against political insurgency had been in place since the turn of the century, and that gave the ruling group the freedom to attack its opponents with a zeal not often seen outside of the South. Consistent with V. O. Key's classic study of black belt counties, there was in Princess Anne a privileged group of conservative whites that was accustomed to rule without accountability and brooked no opposition.[52] This group had maintained a system of racial subordination since colonial times and throughout its long history had demonstrated its willingness to go to great lengths—including violence and the threat of violence—to retain its power.

Throughout the Eastern Shore and Southern Maryland particularly, historians have noted how eighteenth-century governing elites enjoyed the fees of office holding;[53] nineteenth-century "courthouse gangs" enjoyed the benefits of favorable policies of taxation and revenue allocation;[54] and twentieth-century courthouse elites, especially in rural towns, benefited from favorable development policies.[55] Thus political life in Princess Anne is consistent with a well-known pattern, long established in the region. Because Somerset is the southernmost county in Maryland, and very isolated, it was not surprising to find an oligarchy still in power there. The overriding concern of the ruling group did not appear to be the economic welfare of the whole community, but rather to gain personal and economic advantage by maintaining its political dominance and special privileges from the past.

Princess Anne's experience takes on heightened significance when we consider the political upheaval that economic change set in motion. For three hundred years, county courthouse elites had controlled the town government, in spite of the black community's ongoing efforts to restructure the local regime, often with assistance from powerful outside allies. This being so, how can we explain the fact that in 1990, an African American was elected to office there for the first time in history—an event that augured the collapse of the planters' regime?

Historical evidence suggests that it was the inexorable decline of the agricultural sector and the ruling group's reallocation of its economic and political resources into commercial land-use development that precipitated the collapse of the planter class's monopoly of political power. As long as agriculture provided the economic base for the ruling group, it was mainly poor blacks and migrant workers who bore an inordinate share of the costs of production, and neither group had any internal allies who were willing and able to challenge the entrenched power structure. But in the 1980s, when landholding elites began experimenting with commercial and industrial development, they imposed significant social costs on well-educated, white, middle-class outsiders and, in so doing, they provoked an electoral uprising. The case of Princess Anne thus illustrates that profound economic change can prompt human agents to take actions that may eventuate in political as well as economic restructuring. Major economic change should therefore be viewed as a politically and economically disequilibrating event.

Contrary to the Utopian assumptions that undergird most market theories, there was no evidence to suggest that any universal market tendency was guiding this distressed community toward a natural and harmonious restoration of economic or political equilibrium.[56] Those who had much to lose from agriculture's decline deemed it necessary to take whatever actions they could to overcome disequilibria within their private economic domains, but there is no evidence to suggest that the particular strategies they chose were economically determined or in any sense foreordained.

Neither did the governing group's entrepreneurial activities appear to foster the economic welfare of the whole community, although some elites were unmistakably sincere in their belief that the general interest could be served by policies designed to stimulate growth. This was, after all, the dominant ideology at all levels of government during the Reagan era, and, in fairness, let the reader be reminded that, for a while, I too had been persuaded by the simple logic of the market model. But other members of the ruling group manipulated land use for personal gain while proceeding under the ideologically respectable banner of economic development.

In conclusion, the evidence suggests that, while national policy, global economic trends, and ideology exerted strong pressures on this community to find new ways to revitalize the local economy and shore up its tax base, the particular growth policies that Princess Anne adopted should be understood as resulting from the complex interaction of local culture, historical events, and acts of desperation by a contested and crumbling regime.

5

CRISFIELD, 1986–1991

In October, 1987, the city of Crisfield was already reeling from decades of population loss and economic decline when seven local businesses burned to the ground in a late-night fire. But a few months later, when the state of Maryland bestowed 5 million dollars in Community Development Block Grant (CDBG) monies to rebuild the burned-out core of downtown, people wondered if the fire might have been a blessing in disguise.

The urban renewal plan, named Project Phoenix, called for a working artists' center and a range of retail shops where the old Tawes Lumber Yard had once stood. Ample public parking, restrooms, and other infrastructure improvements would be provided to accommodate the estimated twenty-three thousand additional tourists and arts patrons that would be drawn to visit Crisfield annually.[1] But by June 1991, the city had disbursed the full 5 million, and all that was visible to show for it was a parking lot and a public toilet, known to local wags as the "Park and Pee." Needless to say, no increase in tourism resulted.

Historical narrative does not lend itself easily to the telling of what did not happen. Can history be a chronology of nondecisions?[2]

This chapter will explain the community's ambivalence about growth in terms of the disturbance that economic change would create in settled institutions and the kinds of values, both material and intangible, that those institutions continued to serve. In order to explain Crisfield's failure to implement the full plan for Project Phoenix, or any other significant development project in recent years, this chapter will show that the community's social fabric was maintained by conditions and policies that were fundamentally inimical to economic development as usually conceived. In short, it was maintained by a subsistence regime.

An underlying assumption in the analysis that follows is that structures can be explained in terms of an interaction between the desirability of their consequences for different groups and the relative power of those groups. This chapter therefore treats separately each of the four main groups in Crisfield: city hall, the seafood people, the black community, and the chamber. It focuses on their values, policy preferences, and group interests as they saw them.

I have included the roles of prominent individuals in the discussion and the cultural expectations of persons in those roles. This chapter examines the extent to which each person or group was able to influence policy decisions, based on an analysis of the resources they controlled. Because no group was monolithic in social class or ideology, I have also explored variations within groups when relevant to this study.

City Hall

*Add Mayor Scott and Roland Brown to
your list of people who can get their
own way.*[3]

Mayor Richard Scott, known to his constituents as Scotty, was elected in 1986 in a landslide victory, replacing Percy Purnell, "the Chamber's man," who stepped down.[4] It was Scotty's first bid for public office, and the people wanted a change. "The old mayor and city council were arrogant. Their personalities stunk. People were embarrassed and intimidated by them," explained one observer.

But Mayor Scott was widely known and well liked, especially by the poor, and in Crisfield, that meant the majority. He prided himself on not being one of the good ole boys. Scotty grew up poor, and he lacked a high school education. But his humble origins were no disadvantage in Crisfield, for they gave him a sensitivity to people in need. As a former policeman, retired chief of police in Crisfield, and the present head of security at the local hospital, Mayor Scott had often been available to people in times of trouble. He had interpreted the policeman's role as peacemaker and guardian of the people, as well as an agent of social control. Although white, he had strong support in the black community and was known for being especially attentive to the poor.

The mayor's popularity with the common people gave him an independent base of political power, but Scotty had no agenda of his own. Crisfield had never abandoned the eighteenth-century ideal of democratic government, defined by one scholar as "the institutional arrangement for arriving at political decisions which realizes the common good by making the people itself decide issues through the election of individuals who are to assemble in order to carry out its will."[5] Hence the practice of political leadership was more than alien to Crisfielders: it was morally wrong. It was said of J. Millard Tawes, the governor of Maryland who came from Crisfield, that "he was a pristine politician in that he was bound by no convictions that might interfere with his clear reading of public opinion."[6]

Crisfield's elected officials were expected to be faithful to their mandates, and if the mayor had used his office to advance his own policy preferences, the people would have treated it as a usurpation. They viewed the pluralist model of democracy as corrupt for the same reason, and factional politics incurred disapproval whenever it surfaced. The city charter stipulated that ordinances could only be changed or enacted by unanimous vote of the city council. "We iron out our differences before and after the meetings, not in public," explained Mayor Scott, "otherwise people lose respect for government."

Cultural constructions notwithstanding, this analysis recognizes that there was a plurality of interests in Crisfield. On this view, Mayor Scott represented one social element—the city's poor people, both black and white. Scotty understood that "progress," in the form of increasing modernization and economic development, would impose additional hardships on the poor—a point amplified later on. There were other groups in Crisfield nurturing different agendas, however, and they observed the action (or inaction) from the wings.

The city council president, Roland Brown, was second only to Mayor Scott as an influential public official. He taught industrial arts at the middle school, and, as the sole African American elected to public office, his constituency included most of the black community—about one-third of Crisfield's electorate. Some people were pleased that Mayor Scott's sensitivity to black people had been refined through his close association with Roland Brown, his political ally, but others complained that the two men were "racially prejudiced" and intent upon giving everything away to the blacks. Two new city councilmen were elected in 1990, both small businessmen and members of the chamber of commerce. They were often at odds with the mayor and Brown when race was perceived as an issue.

Of the four elected officials in Crisfield, only one, "the Chamber's man," was aggressive in the pursuit of growth. Economic development was threatening to the poor, and to middle-class, small-business owners as well. To both groups, growth meant higher taxes to finance infrastructure improvements and additional services. It meant gentrification, higher property values, more tax increases, tax arrears, foreclosure, and possible eviction. It meant competition for stretched resources, customers, jobs, parking spaces, and crabs.

Crisfielders believed that if they were pitted in competition against wealthy, sophisticated, resourceful, and educated "foreigners" of the kind who already had invaded other counties on the shore, they would lose in intangible as well as material ways. A local journalist explained the intense opposition to an exclusive hunting resort that a developer tried to bring to the area: "They promised they would have jobs for everybody in Somerset County, and we were very excited about that at first, until we realized we would be reduced to a state of servitude to the super rich." Needless to say, the hunting resort was defeated. The people of Crisfield understood that it was possible to be upwardly mobile in material wellbeing and downwardly mobile in status and contentment with life at the same time.

Crisfield was a city so poor that over one-third of the population lived in subsidized public housing.[7] Mayor Scott and Roland Brown both attempted to fulfill the mandate given to them by the poor. In general, they resisted proposals that threatened to extract money from the people in fees and taxes. "Newcomers here are too demanding of city services," the mayor complained, "and that turns people off." They resisted pressure from newcomers and developers alike to extend and professionalize city services and impose more restrictive zoning and building codes. They opposed measures that would add to the burdens of those whose subsistence was already marginal.

Where elected officials aspire to launch major new projects, informal cooperation with business elites is the typical modus operandi.[8] But, like a caretaker regime, a subsistence regime minimizes public expenditure, except for infrastructure maintenance projects that can be financed with state and federal grants.[9] Hence Scotty and Brown enjoyed extraordinary degrees of political freedom. They had a clear mandate, strong electoral support, and no constraining dependence on the business community that might lead them to compromise the general good as they saw it.

It is important to grasp that officials in Crisfield unequivocally supported the goal of replacing the jobs that were lost.[10] Transforming the city into a fancy resort or a tourist mecca was one thing, but stemming population loss and economic decline was another. Layoffs and plant closings happened with ominous frequency during this period, increasing the already swollen ranks of the poor. Thus when Mayor Scott strongly endorsed a proposed maritime industrial park for Crisfield, it was not his aim to foster economic development in the sense of constructing a growth machine. Instead, his goal was to put people back to work. The distinction reveals a profound policy schism.

Again and again this research uncovered a fundamental tension, one could even say an antagonism, between the subsistence goal on the one hand and the development goal on the other.[11] Growth partisans sometimes described city hall as "backward" or "incompetent" because of its failure to rationalize public affairs.[12] But Mayor Scott and Councilor Brown understood all too well the price the majority of residents would pay if community values were sacrificed to the idol of growth.

It is axiomatic in regime theory that "the character of local politics is dependent upon the nature of a community's associational life."[13] This research disclosed that Crisfield's subsistence regime was anchored in strong egalitarian and communitarian values that conflicted with the view that the town should be run like a business firm.

One incident illustrates these continuing tensions. A few days before Christmas 1988, Harvey Hastings, the Princess Anne real estate broker, appeared before Mayor Scott and the Crisfield City Council to make a request on behalf of his client, the owner of the old Arcade movie theatre on Main Street. Hastings petitioned the city to evict a man known as Reverend Best from the premises. The owner wished to sell the crumbling old edifice, but Reverend Best had been living there for some time without water or sewer. Mayor Scott replied that he was unwilling to evict this "nonpaying tenant." He agreed that the city had the authority to do it, but he insisted that some other way of solving the problem had to be found.[14] The mayor explained his philosophy of government to the author as follows: "I'm for the poor people. I don't believe in putting nobody out in the cold. I stand for the right; not the under the table stuff. Honesty prevails. Everybody should have a voice in the government, but usually the little man gets forgotten once somebody's got their vote. It's a sad time when people don't give no thought to their fellow man."[15] Mayor Scott and Councilor Brown were both re-elected for second four-year terms in June 1990. The Crisfield electorate approved the subsistence regime.

FIGURE 5.1 The Old Arcade Theater—Home of Reverend Best

THE SEAFOOD PEOPLE

Packers, pickers, and watermen: these were the seafood people. Although separated by social class, race, and "relation to the means of production," all three groups clung to the status quo. Each group's perceptions of what its real interests were will be examined separately.

The Packers

The packers emerged in the nineteenth century in response to the oystering boom. Their political influence in the city, the county, and the state was, for a time, enormous, until two changes happened that greatly diminished their power. First, the U.S. Supreme Court's 1962 *Baker v. Carr* decision required reapportionment in the states on the basis of the "one man one vote" principle, and thus shifted political power away from the rural counties. When J. Millard Tawes completed his last term of office as governor in 1967, rural and small-town political dominance in Maryland was waning.[16] The power of the packers, as well as the Somerset County planters, from then on was sharply diminished.

The second condition that changed was the decreasing catch in the Bay. The seafood packing houses that still survived in the mid-1980s were hard-pressed to keep their heads above water. They paid black female crab pickers for "piecework," one dollar and seventy-five cents for each pound of crab meat picked, or four dollars and twenty-five cents per hour, whichever was higher. Because no benefits were provided and wages and prices were fixed, paternalistic personality cults developed around the packers, who vied with each other for the loyalties of the workers: "This one buys you supper; that one lets you go home early," explained one informant. "Lending money, helping someone buy a boat, tiding them over until the season started, taking care of the people who work for you" is what gave them control, he averred.

The packers opposed every major development project considered for Crisfield during this five-year study. They opposed the maritime industrial park that Mayor Scott fought for, claiming that increased boat traffic would disturb their crab shedding operations. They opposed Project Phoenix, explaining that they would be subjected to endless complaints about seafood odors from the owners of new yuppie hotels and townhouses. One packer testified that he would be forced constantly to defend himself against tourist shop owners who were "likely to object to industrial activities."[17]

When the U.S. Corps of Engineers declined to authorize dredging the harbor, and thus killed Crisfield's hopes for a maritime industrial park, some leading citizens believed that the packers had influenced state and federal officials, as in former days. This research uncovered no evidence that gave credence to these suspicions, but, in the minds of the people, at least, the packers still had political power of mythical dimensions. This construction of reality was expressed by a small-business owner:

> The seafood packers held down development of this town for years. Criscraft wanted to come in and they stopped it cold. The seafood people have never wanted any industry that would bring in seven dollars an hour; they would lose all their workers. Everybody goes along with the bigwigs, even if it hurts them. They control everything with money—they always have—and there's no way you can accomplish anything or change anything if they don't want it. They would go higher than city government; it would come down the chain; it would hurt you. No businessman ever dared run for office in this town until 1990. They knew if they stepped on the toes of the bigwigs they would be ruined.

Whatever the real extent of the packers' power might have been at the time of this research, it is certain that this group viewed development as inimical to its interests, but not for the reasons given in public. One packer stated the truth of the matter bluntly, confiding that the only reason he had been able to stay in business was because the Economic Development Commission had failed. If the EDC had succeeded in attracting outside industry into the county, he would not have been able to compete with a higher wage, and he would have gone under.[18]

The Pickers

Seasonal piecework in the seafood industry was a major source of employment for blacks in the city. One-third of the population lived in "the projects," and 75 percent of those families were seasonally employed as oyster shuckers or crab pickers and wrappers. In 1990, there were only two nonseafood-related industries in Crisfield.[19]

By tradition, crab pickers and wrappers were black women or male homosexuals; oyster shuckers were men. In recent times, a few white women have also worked as pickers and wrappers. Because picking crabs requires manual dexterity, prestige accrued to the fastest workers. The community honored the winners of its annual crab-picking contest. Pickers worked in the summer months only, and the smaller group of oyster shuckers worked in the winter. Both groups collected unemployment compensation the rest of the year and often Aid for Families with Dependent Children (AFDC) as well. It was frequently said that the pickers were content with this way of life and not eager to alter their modus vivendi.

FIGURE 5.3 Crab Pickers in Crisfield

While the statement that economically dependent pieceworkers were satisfied tends to arouse skepticism in reform-minded scholars, a close examination of the economic realities renders the notion more plausible. First, because skilled crab pickers could earn up to one hundred dollars a day, they could earn as much working six months a year in the crab-picking season as working the year around for minimum wage.[20] Thus in income alone, they were better off receiving for six months' work what they might otherwise earn in twelve.

Additionally, seasonal workers lived in the projects managed by the Crisfield Housing Authority, rated the best in the nation for its size.[21] In this community, to reside in subsidized housing carried no stigma. In fact, blacks and whites competed to get into the projects. "It's not fair that 80 to 90 percent of the residents of public housing are black," one city councilor complained. "There are whites that need it but can't get in. That's unfair." The councilor's figures were grossly exaggerated. In 1991, only 56 percent of the units were occupied by black families.[22]

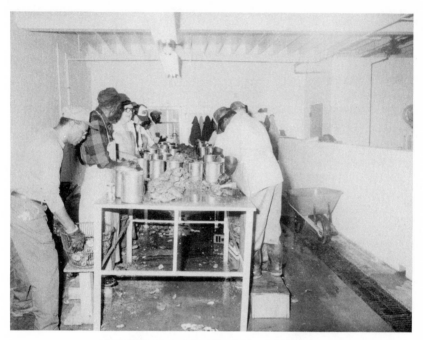

FIGURE 5.3 Oyster Shuckers in Crisfield

One can speculate that economic development would expand opportunities for these workers and offer them a chance to break their dependence on entitlement programs. After all, it is said that a rising tide lifts all ships. One can inveigh against the exploitation of a powerless and dependent people and argue that any job offering escape from these conditions would be more dignified, just, and humane than the status quo. But that would be to superimpose one's cultural worldview upon people who see it otherwise, and the aim of this study is to explain how Crisfielders' preferences were formed, not someone else's. An African American employment official explained:

FIGURE 5.4 A Seafood Worker Taking Maryland Blue Crabs
from a Steamer

Being laid off is not as traumatic here as in other places. This is a family-oriented area that is used to seasonal work. Families hang together here and take each other in. Industries that come here, attracted by the cheap work force, that pay only minimum wage, are disappointed when they try to exploit the situation, because workers leave them as soon as the seasonal work becomes available. The ambitious people of both races leave for better opportunities elsewhere, which means that those who stay are pretty well satisfied with this way of life.

Few seasonal workers appeared to believe that the kinds of industries that the EDC was attempting to recruit would provide them with jobs that would either enhance their lives or embellish their fortunes. If any selectivity was being exercised at all by the EDC, it was to select enterprises so odious that no other locality would want them.[23] If the crab pickers were rational actors, and we assume that they were, it is entirely plausible that they preferred seasonal piecework supplemented by entitlement programs. The only realistic alternative available to them, as they saw it, was permanent employment under sweat-shop conditions, without child care or benefits, at a loss of real income, because that was the kind of employment that the EDC tried to attract.

Realistically, this might have been the only kind of industry that considered locating in Somerset County, given its relative isolation, its substandard infrastructure, and the exceptionally low level of education, especially in Crisfield. But even if jobs of a more desirable sort should materialize, experience with the prison had taught the poor people that the good jobs would not go to them.[24] Crisfielders' expectations, based on experience, were that outsiders would be recruited for the better positions.

The people were dubious about the benefits of economic development, not only because it failed to hold out realistic hope for genuine opportunities, as it was practiced, but there were positive disincentives that attached to the idea as well. First, if a permanent job became available to a seasonal worker, no matter how poorly compensated it was or how onerous the terms and conditions of employment, the worker would be disqualified to receive off-season unemployment compensation if, its having been deemed "suitable" by a case worker, he or she refused to accept the position. Furthermore, if many job openings of this kind had become available, forcing seasonal workers out of the industry in large numbers, people felt that the seafood industry would have been seriously jeopardized, as already reported.

Even from a purely economic standpoint, it is frankly difficult to imagine that many people in Crisfield would have been better off if the precarious seafood industry had gone under. Because, in spite of its anachronistic labor relations and its marginal earnings, it was still the mainstay of Crisfield's economy, not to mention its way of life since time immemorial. If that industry collapsed, one must wonder what would come to Crisfield to replace it: Can we interest you in a medical waste storage facility? May we offer you a contaminated soil incinerator? When all of these many considerations are pondered, it becomes understandable that neither the packers nor the pickers were deeply desirous of changing the status quo.

The Watermen

Chapter 3 described how the watermen felt about modernizing forces, tourism, and growth; there is no need to further expound on it here. Suffice it to say that they, like the packers, opposed every important plan for development in Crisfield, including the deep water port, the industrial park, and Project Phoenix.[25] "They are a single-issue interest group with a moral charter, they think, to protect their God-given right to plunder the bay," said one state official.

Nobody wanted to go up against the watermen. They were not politically active, as a rule, until their ox was gored. Then they turned out by the hundreds, unified, passionate, and colorfully articulate with their residual Elizabethan inflections and figures of speech. When they learned to use public hearings with style and dramatic effect in the 1980s, they emerged as a political force to contend with both at state and at national levels.

Whether packers, pickers, or watermen, very few of the seafood people desired economic development. Of the three groups whose way of life depended upon the seafood industry, the watermen and the seafood packers wielded sufficient political power to have an effect upon policy outcomes.

THE BLACK COMMUNITY

The black people have it made. They
live in fine housing and work only
six months a year. [26]

Older members of the black community in Crisfield reported that conditions for African Americans had deteriorated unbelievably in the last few decades. By far the largest social class was the poor. These were the seasonal workers, the laborers, the elderly, and the unemployed. The economic status of Crisfield's black working class was largely tied to the seafood industry, and, as the catch in the bay declined, poverty and desperation increased. Many women still found seasonal work in the crab picking houses, but in ever dwindling numbers, and black men were desperate for work. "Social Services can't support everybody in town who needs a living," one black minister stated. Some people found employment outside of the county, but for most, this was not a realistic option. Jobs were scarce in the entire lower shore region. Furthermore, Somerset County had no public transportation. Increasingly, blacks were sustained by underground economies in drugs and theft, but, so were some in the white community, including the chief of police, who later was convicted on three counts of theft.[27]

There were no black-owned businesses in the county, except a few beer parlors and snack bars. The entrepreneurial spirit that had characterized the community of free blacks during earlier historical periods had long since been extinguished because of the unavailability of investment capital and credit to African Americans. The middle class was made up largely of professionals serving the black community, preachers, and educators employed in the county school system. Those who had government jobs with the state or the county enjoyed a level of economic security that was unknown to anyone else in the black community.

Obviously there was room for improvement in the conditions of life for Crisfield's African American population. Spokespersons for various groups in the black community consistently disclosed a range of suppressed policy concerns. Two such issues deserve exploration. First, even a minimal public transportation system would have brought gainful employment within reach of significant numbers of people, black and white, wanting jobs. But the ruling elites, whether seafood packers or growers, had no interest in transporting "their" labor pool out of the county for higher wages.[28] And second, as desirable as public housing was in the eyes of both races in Crisfield, most people would have preferred owning their own homes to living as public dependents under the supervision of a white "overseer."

This issue warrants elaboration. Black home ownership had diminished inexorably over the decades in Crisfield, as elsewhere in Somerset County. Black people's homes had been seized, one by one, for nonpayment of property taxes. An entire black neighborhood, called "Turf," was razed in the 1970s to make room for an industrial park that was never developed.[29] Today, Turf is an open field, full of high grass. "They demolished a viable community there," Councilor Brown lamented. "Like a fool, I went along with it at the time, convincing people to give up their homes, to my ever-lasting regret. Afterwards, I attended council meetings to hold their feet to the fire to build the new houses that were promised, but nothing happened. I haven't forgotten," he added.

Jobs, transportation, business opportunities, and housing were but a few of the items on the latent policy agenda that were handled by nondecision making. With so many matters of concern to the downtrodden minority left unaddressed and racial injustices salting the wounds of the poor, the fact that so small a number of blacks showed an interest in public affairs requires some explaining.

The black people's lack of interest in local government can be assigned to two factors: First, there was a sense of futility—a belief that their political efforts would be, at best, unavailing. The second reason was the widespread fear of "upsetting the apple cart." This innocuous-sounding metaphor disguised a sinister portent in its meaning. Grasping it requires a fuller examination of a concept introduced in earlier chapters—the structure for social control that involved "system blacks."

The "system" referred to the system of white caste dominance that prevailed throughout Somerset County, and system blacks were those who were seemingly willing to be used by the system to perpetuate racial subordination. The long view of Somerset's history reveals that the ruling group adjusted the means of subordination to change with the times, and the cooptation of black leaders was the primary method used in the modern era.[30] A local black scholar explained it this way: "The system has perfected itself over the centuries to where it can lift you up or cast you down. Outsiders can succeed only if they are tested and tried by the insiders. The system has groomed blacks to keep other blacks in line."

Blacks advanced by signaling that they would not challenge the system of white caste dominance or attempt to mobilize a black constituency. Selected individuals were elevated to high positions and rewarded with generous salaries, social status, and power, and they mediated between the black community and the ruling group. These were the system blacks. Recall that Dwayne Whittington, Jr., superintendent of schools for Somerset County, was, by reputation, foremost among them and that City Councilor Roland Brown, as a teacher in the Woodson Middle School, was his subordinate. While Brown himself was not viewed as a system black, some people believed there were issues that he could not tackle as an elected official without jeopardizing his job in the county school system.

Another example of how the system worked involved William P. Hytche, chancellor of UMES. Like Whittington, Hytche was widely perceived in the African American community as a system black. Recall that Kirkland Hall, the president of the local chapter of the NAACP, was also the university's athletics director. As such, he was under Hytche's authority. And, as in Councilor Brown's case, people wondered how free Hall was to challenge the system. These relationships appear to be classic examples of power imparted by anticipated reactions. A hierarchical structure that gave Somerset County's ruling elites the power to discipline black leaders and black elected officials through their intermediaries, the system blacks, was firmly in place. One can only imagine how chilling the effect was.

The black community's latent policy agenda required action at town, county, state, and federal levels, as much of it was beyond the scope and authority of the town government. But, except for voting, political participation by blacks was negligible for reasons that have now become clear: to upset the apple cart was to challenge the policies and practices of the ruling group and thus bring renewed repression upon the black community. The ancient taboos against bucking white caste dominance and fomenting political insurgency still prevailed in the late 1980s.

The high level of racial intimidation in Somerset County presented real difficulties in executing this research. The reluctance of blacks to grant interviews seemed to reflect an understandable distrust of whites and fear of reprisals. Even so, the courage of those who dared to speak dangerous truths to a stranger revealed the existence of a redemptive hope. "The church here keeps the people alive spiritually so that they can survive under these conditions," explained one informant. The church was the most treasured resource of the black community, because it provided "renewal in the spirit above and beyond human ability to affect change."[31]

THE CHAMBER

Those who are active in economic
development are active in
real estate. [32]

In Crisfield, conversations that touched upon the politics of economic development usually included some mention of the good-ole-boy system, defined by a local observer as "basically the Chamber." By this, he meant the Crisfield Area Chamber of Commerce. More exactly, the expression referred to an elite group of leaders within the chamber. Therefore, to avoid confusing the good ole boys with the general membership of the chamber of commerce, I will henceforth refer to them as the inner chamber.

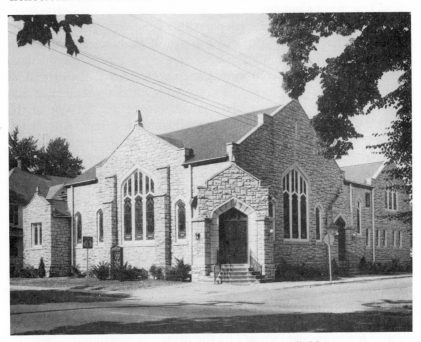

FIGURE 5.5 A Black Church in Crisfield

By reputation, the members of the inner chamber included these six men: James Dodson, a restaurant owner, developer, and entrepreneur; Charles McClenahan, the president of an insurance agency; Harry T. Phoebus, Jr., a lawyer and son of the late Maryland Senator Harry T. Phoebus; Scott Tawes, CPA, an insurance agency owner, developer, Crisfield city auditor, and grandson of Governor J. Millard Tawes; Jay Tawes, a real estate broker, developer, EDC chairman, and a member of the extended family of the governor; Robert Wilson, a real estate broker, developer, and president of the chamber of commerce. The policy preferences of this group were straightforward: they wanted to turn Crisfield into a growth machine.

According to Molotch's growth machine thesis, land interests control local government. We have seen, however, that this was not so in Crisfield, which had been controlled for a hundred years by the antigrowth seafood packers, and, in the mid1980s, by a combination of antigrowth and controlled-growth interests that maintained a subsistence regime.

The inner chamber understood that achievement of its development goals required the cooperation of the city, and to that end Harry T. Phoebus, Jr., initiated a series of chamber breakfasts for elected officials. The idea was to create a forum for dialogue between the business community and public bodies. In Crisfield, as in other small towns, most businessmen favored a caretaker or subsistence regime that kept taxes down. Hence the purpose of the breakfasts was twofold. In addition to the obvious aim of gaining the city's cooperation with its development goals, the inner chamber hoped that by sponsoring a series of friendly discussions with proponents of the subsistence regime in an open forum, they could convert the majority of the chamber's members to their progrowth agenda.

When city hall and the chamber came together on these occasions and explored their different views face to face, two different worldviews came into collision, revealing the schism (perhaps I should say chasm, so great were their differences) referred to above. For illustration, the following section reports what occurred at the chamber breakfast on June 17, 1989, attended by the author. On that occassion, Mayor Scott, two city councilors, and the town manager responded to questions posed by the master of ceremonies, Harry T. Phoebus, Jr., an engaging and popular man. On that Saturday morning, James Scott's *homo peasanticus* was courteously questioned by *homo oeconomicus*.[33] Their dialogue illuminates the cultural barriers to economic development that confronted the would-be architects of a growth machine.

The Chamber Breakfast

Attending the breakfast were Mayor Richard Scott, Councilor Allison Milbourne, Councilor Larry Tyler, and Town Manager Juke Tyler, Larry's brother. When the dishes were cleared away, "Harry T" rose to his feet and posed six questions to the officials.

The first question regarded rezoning Maryland and Richardson avenues, the only two roads into town. Phoebus said it had been suggested that both should be rezoned commercial, and he asked what city hall's view of the matter was. Only the mayor responded, and his answer was brief: "The people who live there would have a fit, including me! What is your next question, please?" (He evidently viewed land in terms of its "use value" only, its "exchange value" not having entered his mindset.)

The next question pertained to the view that a ban on storage barns on Main Street should be imposed, because they were not the "highest and best use of the land." Looking puzzled, the mayor queried: "Storage barns? What's wrong with storage barns? I declare, I have never heard a single complaint about a storage barn! Next question." (This was the mandate theory of democracy, implicitly expressed.)

Third, some people felt that the city should be building sidewalks. Was any progress being made on that front? Juke Tyler responded, "Nope, can't afford to."

The mayor added, "We oppose raising taxes for that." Then a lengthy discussion ensued about whether city hall should hire a grant specialist to help obtain federal sidewalk grants.

Fourth, the chamber wanted to know what was being done to curb the drug traffic in Crisfield, which was increasing, they thought. "Nothing," replied the mayor. "We don't have any police manpower to spare from their regular duties. Citizens have to help out by reporting license plates. Everybody should pitch in to help out the police."

The fifth question referred to a large parcel of waterfront property, beyond the marina, that was owned by the city. Phoebus inquired how that land would be used. Juke Tyler answered that the city council and the mayor had approved a subsidized housing project for the site. With that, Bob Wilson, realtor and president of the chamber, seemed to choke on his eggs, then he rose from his chair, remonstrating with the officials: "The most valuable land in Crisfield is going for *subsidized housing! That is inefficient use of a prime location!*" In fact, the land in question was reclaimed marsh, filled in decades earlier by HUD for the restricted purpose of creating a site for subsidized housing.

Others objected that "Those people don't pay taxes," "There's no need for more low-rent housing," and "If you increase the supply in Somerset County, those people will migrate here from Wicomico."

The mayor responded that the project was already underway. There was a need and a long waiting list and "anybody is welcome to come look over the plans and the figures; nothing is being done in secret. You're welcome to come and see for yourself any time."

When the room had calmed down, Phoebus described a suggested revision to the city charter that would allow nonresidents who owned businesses in town to run for office, and then he politely inquired what his guests' reactions might be. Councilor Milbourne, an elementary school principal, smiled as he answered:

> I personally would oppose that, Sir. Let me explain why. My apologies to the ladies present, but if you want to govern us, you've got to sleep with us. There are values and concerns in this community that are not commercial. And I have no reason to think that just because someone owns and operates a business here they would be aware of and sensitive to those concerns. So my position is as I've said: If you want to govern us, you'll have to sleep with us, and I would oppose any motion to allow nonresidents of this city to run for office.

The breakfast adjourned shortly thereafter.

If the inner chamber hoped, by this method, to convert city hall to its aggressive progrowth agenda, there was little evidence that it was succeeding. While there was no lack of goodwill on either side, to say that the two groups talked past each other is an understatement, given their different worldviews. Perhaps the aim of converting the rest of the chamber's membership was more successful, but the impact of these discourses paled in the light of events that bore promise of being far more persuasive.

Plant Closings

"Already stunned by recent news that the Carvel Hall cutlery plant may close at the end of September, Somerset County is now reeling following notice that the Mrs. Paul's Kitchens in Crisfield and the Campbell Soup plant in Pokomoke City will close around March 1, affecting over 500 workers," announced the *Somerset Herald* on August 30, 1989. Mayor Scott responded in his characteristic way. With the individual, as always, at the forefront of his attention, he offered his sympathy to the people who had just lost their jobs, then went on to say, "This is a perfect example of why we need the maritime park."[34]

Meanwhile, the chamber arranged a hasty visit from Governor Schaefer. One week later, the governor arrived with an entourage of state officials, and they toured the three plants, making speeches. "An irritated Gov. William Donald Schaefer told local officials . . . 'you must pull yourselves up by your bootstraps' . . . and Crisfield 'can do more,' . . ." the *Somerset Herald* reported.[35]

Then the chamber convened what it called a "crisis summit," in which "22 company, chamber, city, county, and state officials" met for discussions in hopes of starting a process of "pulling together."[36] Next, Scott Tawes and the mayor created the Economic Development Task Force, pursuant to the governor's exhortations, and Tawes was named chair. Its goal, he said, was "to spur economic development for the lower end of Somerset County."[37]

This group soon produced a list of development goals and presented it to the public, the city of Crisfield, and the governor.[38] Of primary importance, the Tawes task force concluded, was "an updated city planning program for Crisfield, which would take efficient land use into account."[39] The inner chamber was, by then, firmly in charge of the process. Jay Tawes, this time as chair of the chamber's economic committee, undertook to review the city planning document and develop a new one, with the help of professional consultants.

The Business Forum

On October 25, 1990, Douglas H. Wilson, a consultant in strategic planning and marketing from nearby Salisbury, conducted a brainstorming session in the Crisfield Fire House on behalf of the chamber. Called the "Business Forum," this gathering's purpose was to involve the whole community in the process of developing a new city plan. The consultant engaged all of the participants in the process, drawing out their views about Crisfield's assets and its barriers to growth and their ideas and preferences regarding how to revitalize their city. He then sent a written report to Jay Tawes, which included his recommendations, based on the ideas expressed at the Business Forum.

The details of Wilson's recommendations need not be repeated. More germane is the disappointment that he expressed in the process. Because there were no representatives of the black community or the seafood industry in attendance at the Business Forum, he cautioned Tawes with regard to the plan: "It cannot be seen as an endeavor of a narrow segment of the community who will be its sole benefactor. In order to succeed, the plan must be vigorously and visibly supported by all segments, and therefore, all segments must be involved in the process. Failure to generate this support and enthusiasm will severely diminish the plan's effectiveness."[40]

In keeping with Wilson's predictions, the plan failed to gain city hall's approval. The chamber asked Councilor Kim Lawson, who was one of its members, to form a committee to work out their differences and act as a liaison between the two bodies. But when this research was concluded, one year later, nothing had come of it.

Summary

"The Chamber is an interest group with no interest at all in the poor and their housing problems," said one observer. This perception of the inner chamber was shared by others in Crisfield. Even some of the regular membership of the chamber saw the inner chamber in this light. One well-respected small businessman said, "People in the insurance business, the real estate business—99 percent of the time there's a big push to bring something in here, it's for their own personal gain, not the good of the community. They're lining their pockets." Spokespersons for the black community and the seafood people expressed similar sentiments.

The people of Crisfield, on the whole, did not respect power or money. To the contrary, while they did not lack respect for Harry T. Phoebus, Jr., and other individuals, they resented the "bigwigs" and "good ole boys" in general, just as the original watermen had resented the haughty tobacco planters in days of old. Therefore, prestige did not accompany membership in the inner chamber, except in the elite strata of the county and state, outside of Crisfield, where their networks extended. To whatever degree they enjoyed political power in Crisfield, it seemed to derive largely from their institutional affiliations and connections with outside elites.

CONCLUSION

Crisfield, in the 1980s, was a town in severe economic distress that refused to be transformed into a growth machine. A former EDC director described Mayor Scott and his program thus: "He is a fine and decent human being, a humble man who loves his city. He opposes zoning and building codes because to restrict mobile homes or condemn somebody's dilapidated houses might hurt somebody. It might leave somebody homeless." By maintaining a subsistence regime, Scotty was faithful to his mandate from Crisfield's majority, which was made up of poor whites, blacks, small businessmen, and seafood people.

This chapter's general aim was to show how policy preferences regarding economic development were "embedded in concrete, ongoing systems of social relations."[41] In Crisfield, these way-of-life factors produced a subsistence regime that impeded economic development efforts. There were social, economic, and political structures in place that prevented the city from yeilding to the pressure of land-based business elites, or "modern rentiers," as Logan and Molotch have called them.[42]

The local culture was another factor that militated against economic development. When this research was conducted in the late 1980s, Crisfield was still, in essence, a watermen's town, and most of the people who lived there shared in the watermen's mindset. Isolationism continued to be a prominent feature of their worldview. Perhaps the oystering boom's grim lessons remained embedded in Crisfielders' culture or collective unconscious, for they seemed as aware as any social scientist could be of the destruction that unbridled market forces could wreak on the social fabric of their town.[43]

One may never know all of the reasons why Project Phoenix was not implemented as planned. On the surface, the main obstacle was that the Tawes family (not including Scott or Jay Tawes) was reportedly unwilling to sell the Tawes Lumber Yard to the city and therefore demanded a completely unreasonable price. The artists' studios and small shops that were supposed to have been constructed on that site were the project's central attraction. The lumber yard was thus the linchpin of the whole plan, and when the city failed to acquire it, the project collapsed.

The use of eminent domain was, theoretically, an option; but from a social and cultural standpoint, it was out of the question. An official explained that one could not seize a man's property against his will and continue to live in the same town with him, his family, and his friends. "Sometime you might need one of 'em to fix your car," as he put it. City hall was apparently unwilling to alienate the extended Tawes family, and thus Project Phoenix was doomed. The remaining Community Development Block Grant monies were reallocated for sidewalks, sewers, and other projects.

Some people suspected that an influential seafood packer had sabotaged Project Phoenix by insuring that would-be developers could not obtain financing from local banks. Others speculated that the problem lay with the project's manager, Tony Bruce, who, although he was the city solicitor, was not widely trusted in Crisfield. While this study suggests that such theories are plausible, they cannot be verified by the empirical evidence. However, with or without exact knowledge of the proximate causes of Project Phoenix's undoing, the whole episode takes on a larger meaning when one considers how many of the local people, including the most powerful seafood packers, viewed development projects as endangering their interests and their way of life.

Crisfield was based in a maritime economy rather than a land-based economy, and this led to social structures and a culture that had extensive implications for economic-development policy. It was of critical importance that the anticipated reactions of the powerful seafood packers, who opposed growth as inimical to their interests, had, until 1990, discouraged the community's land-based business elites from running for public office. The packers themselves had rarely aspired to hold office, preferring the greater flexibility that pressing the levers of power in private afforded. As benificent patrons, they lent money, advanced supplies until the season started, and in various other ways kept workers and suppliers dependent upon them and in their debt in the manner of Southern cotton brokers.[44] Much of their power was thus based on a highly paternalistic structure of labor relations that sometimes bordered on debt peonage. Furthermore, their *perceived* power was almost unlimited. The result was that people in the community took care not to step on their toes.

The watermen were arrayed on the side of the packers with regard to economic development, and they too wielded significant political power. It is important to note that their antigrowth preferences cannot be reduced to material self-interest. Viewing themselves as a romantic, dying breed, they opposed growth in order to protect, at least for the span of their lifetimes, a unique, independent way of life on the water. They were sure that growth would hasten its impending demise.[45]

This case study shows that there were fundamental conflicts between water-based and land-based interests, which powerfully differentiated the preferences of individuals with regard to growth policies. Another conclusion to be drawn from Crisfield's experience is that economic maximization cannot be the prevailing principal in a social order in which subsistence concerns predominate, because it requires taking risks and investing slack resources, neither of which is feasible for people who live on the margin.[46]

FIGURE 5.6 The Skipjack: An Antique Sailing Vessel Still Used
by Watermen in Somerset County

Small businessmen in Crisfield were wary of growth for reasons that were both economic and social. They did not believe they
could survive in business if they were forced to compete with
national retail chains, for example; and neither did they relish having their roles in the civic life of the community, and their contributions, displaced and belittled by an influx of wealthy outsiders.
Thus even the general membership in the chamber of commerce
was ambivalent about growth. The majority of the people in
Crisfield were without extra material resources, whether small
businessmen or poor blacks and whites, and these were the people
that city hall represented by maintaining a subsistence regime.

While some of the poor had policy concerns that included
enlarging their social and economic opportunities, these concerns
were, for the most part, politically suppressed at the county level.
Crisfield's elected officials, such as Mayor Scott and Councilor
Brown, were responsive to these constituencies, but their responses
tended to be highly personalized and therefore unlikely to affect sys-

temic change.[47] Furthermore, the town government had sharply limited powers and resources.

Continuing systems of racial subordination and the remnant of a white agricultural oligarchy that operated in the county accounted for much of the nondecision making. Somerset's large farmers and seafood packers both had a historical interest in maintaining a large supply of cheap surplus labor, thus amenities such as public transportation, which would have allowed the poor to seek higher wages outside of the county, had never been sought by the county's ruling elites.

Even though the modern rentiers that dominated the Crisfield Area Chamber of Commerce were very aggressive in their pursuit of development, they were unable to transform the city into a growth machine. On the county and state levels, they may have enjoyed some prestige and access to political elites, but in Crisfield their power was offset by the countervailing power of the seafood people. The general populace viewed the growth machine partisans in the chamber as a small group of arrogant "haves" that preyed upon "have nots." It was said, for example, that they were "out to line their pockets." The expression itself reveals the disapproval with which profit maximization was viewed in the local culture.

The anticipated reactions of the seafood packers kept the business community from seeking positions of leadership in the local government, which was another reason market mores never became well established in Crisfield. Values were shaped instead by the subsistence requirements of a poor population, paternalistic social structures, and historical experience.

6

CONCLUSION

It was clear from the outset of this study that Somerset County did not conform to the market model that dominated the field of public policy analysis in the 1980s. What was not clear was how to explain this deviation from widely accepted economic theories. Following the "social embeddedness argument," I assumed that the policy preferences of individuals were powerfully shaped by local history, culture, and social structures. Hence the present research required an analysis of how these way-of-life variables shaped both individual preferences and public policy decisions in Princess Anne and Crisfield. The need to investigate how policy decisions were made becomes clear when we consider the fact that, even within the same community, individual preferences regarding economic development varied.

There is an advantage to using urban regime theory as a framework for this kind of research, which is that it directs our attention to the informal governing arrangements that are key to understanding policy making. There was a disadvantage, however, that I encountered in using it for this study, which relates to its focus on large cities and the fact that it has little to say about traditional social structures and cultural values. It became necessary, then, to extend this theoretical framework in order to incorporate the structural and cultural variables that intellectual convention has relegated to rural communities only. I have thus attempted to transcend the urban-rural duality by positing a new theoretical synthesis that will be useful to scholars investigating the political economy of human settlements of all sizes. If we apply this model comparatively, we can begin to apprehend the full range of factors that impinge upon economic development. We can also begin to sort out the conditions under which different sociocultural and political variables are likely to have different effects. Princess Anne and Crisfield are only the first leg of the journey. Still, they afford important insights and a number of implications for economic development policy.

SUMMARY OF THE FINDINGS

The present research reveals that the social structure of Somerset County was complex enough to contain opposing tendencies in its two sectors. The growth machine that was constructed in Princess Anne and the subsistence regime that was maintained in Crisfield could not have resulted from the operation of inexorable economic laws. History shows that the difference between the two towns resulted from the cultural bifurcation that occurred in the early seventeenth century, when two different economies became established in the Chesapeake region, one land-based and hierarchical, the other water-based and cooperative. The remarkably different ways of life in Princess Anne and Crisfield stem from their unique histories and different economies: hence their different development policies.

Possibly this study's most significant finding is that because specific types of economies can sustain certain ways of life and not others, individuals correctly viewed economic change as a potentially restructuring event. Many citizens had the foresight to realize that growth threatens to disrupt long established power relations, degrade cultural values, and upset delicately balanced subsistence arrangements. Their reactions to proposed development projects were therefore predicated upon their informal assessments of the likely sociocultural impacts of those projects and how their own values, preferences, and political and economic interests would be affected. This largely depended upon the place of the individual in the social order. Let us re-examine some of the social and political ramifications of economic development policy in the two towns.

FIGURE 6.1 Meeting for Breakfast in the Washington Hotel Dining Room

Princess Anne

Princess Anne, because it was the county seat and the commercial center for Somerset's agricultural industry, was the headquarters for what is referred to here as the "planters' regime." Historians refer to the planters' oligarchies that dominated Maryland's Eastern Shore counties as "courthouse elites" or "courthouse gangs."[1] But in the mid-1980s, when the townspeople of Princess Anne spoke of the collection of exclusively white male insiders who met in the back of the Washington Hotel dining room every Saturday morning for breakfast and decided the fate of the town and county, they called it the "good-ole-boy machine." This element controlled most of the county throughout most of its history. The social order that it perpetuated was hierarchical, and social relations were characterized by pronounced political, economic, and race inequalities.

But the black community, which constituted the majority of the population in Princess Anne in 1990, had long desired change, and because of the severe decline in agriculture, the good ole boys were prepared to accept change as well. There was an ongoing, bitter struggle, however, over exactly what the terms of the change were to be. Chapter 4 detailed some of the more recent forms that this struggle took.

Elite dominance in Somerset County had been perpetuated since colonial times by structures that endowed certain groups with the lion's share of political power and economic advantage. Because most people in these communities lived close to the subsistence margin, the few who controlled the resources that enabled others to secure a livelihood were often able to shape the choices of those who depended upon them. This is not to imply a deliberate strategy on the part of the privileged groups necessarily, but rather a structural tendency. Consider the following conception of how preferences are formed.

Scholars have argued that people are not generally motivated to attain the best of all possible worlds, but that their preferences are shaped instead by the limited opportunities presented in the situation at hand: "In other words, people go for what looks attainable."[2] The large landowners in the Princess Anne vicinity (and, starting with the oystering boom, the seafood packers in Crisfield) were in a position to define much of what was and was not attainable for members of economically dependent or subordinate groups, such as seasonal workers and blacks. Because these structures, to a large extent, were maintained by virtue of the social and material inducements controlled by elites, individual and group behavior was indirectly regulated in a way that tended to perpetuate inequalities. Call this the "power theory" of preference formation.

Additionally, paternalistic social structures inculcated a worldview that included meanings, values, and expectations, hence they had a strong conservative influence on the local culture. The system for perpetuating race subordination that involved the cooptation of black leaders is a telling example of this, for it promoted an attitude of moral complacency and racial bigotry in the white population, and it fostered an opportunistic approach to life in some African Americans and a submissive stance in others. The "system" was thus reinforced by the mindsets that it instilled in both races. Indeed, the Southern mind was "a mighty bulwark" for the preservation of the Southern political and racial status quo, as Cash long ago observed.[3] Structures tended therefore to be self-perpetuating until challenged by instigating events.

Somerset County's social order was threatened by potentially restructuring events at various times in its history. Chapter 5 identifies several periods of possible regime transformation, such as the American Revolution, the Civil War, and the civil rights movement. But the historical evidence reveals that the democratic social change that might have occurred during these periods of regime crisis invariably was thwarted, sometimes by a resort to violence. Thus, even when change was supported by external trends and events, local elites succeeded in perpetuating their rule and making good their motto *semper eadem* (ever the same).

By the arbitrary and paternalistic use of the resources and offices they controlled, the ruling group had managed always to salvage and adjust the social structures that supported their privileged position. Except in the watermen's communities, which composed a separate society, it was still understood in the 1980s that individuals from certain families were "born to govern," as one observer expressed it, and that this oligarchy brooked no opposition.

Informants reported that, in the aftermath of the civil rights demonstrations and riots that occurred in the 1960s, most of Princess Anne's courthouse elites went into seclusion on country estates, but, because the town charter still gave the franchise to nonresident property owners, this did not mean that they had relinquished control of the town. The severe decline in agriculture in recent decades was another potentially restructuring event, because it undermined the economic foundations of this regime. Thus by the 1980s, the town was surrounded by increasingly unremunerative farmland and experiencing fiscal distress, and, at the same time, the governing group was searching for a new economic base. In 1986, the timely appearance of Harvey Hastings, the real estate broker, provided informal leadership in constructing a new growth machine. This group then tried to reap personal profit through commercial development of the land. Princess Anne's development policy can therefore be understood as the governing group's somewhat desperate attempt to shift to a new economic base without surrendering its political dominance.

FIGURE 6.2 Celebrating "Old Princess Anne Days" at the Teakle Mansion

But in an unanticipated turn of events, this policy led directly to the electoral uprising of 1990 and the eventual collapse of the large landowners' monopoly of political power. It was the naive readiness of middle-class newcomers to challenge the traditional power structure, in response to the debasement of "use values" that the growth machine perpetrated on the town, that provided a window of opportunity for Princess Anne's black majority to elect a representative to the town government for the first time in history. These events demonstrate the complex interactions among economic, social, and political processes.

Crisfield

Crisfield, by contrast, was founded by dissidents and marginal persons who fled in defiance of the plantation hierarchy and established a separate regime in the waterways that border the Chesapeake Bay. "South county" was a self-contained society from earliest times and markedly different from the rest of the county along several dimensions. The watermen's communities have always been "in the county but not of it." This is not to say that they were completely untouched by the social order that prevailed further inland, but these forces were mitigated by the structure and worldview that was generated by their own unique history—a remarkably different history from Princess Anne's.

Crisfield's response to economic decline in the late 1980s was based on the subsistence needs of its poor population and was fundamentally at odds with the development goals of the Crisfield Area Chamber of Commerce, which, contrary to the growth machine thesis, had little influence in city hall. Mayor Richard Scott was a poor man who lacked education—a Populist who generated a phenomenal trust. (In Princess Anne, by contrast, clouds of suspicion hung over the town like the clam plant's malodorous fumes.) Notwithstanding the racism that pervaded the culture in both places, blacks had a civic presence in Crisfield that they lacked in Princess Anne, where, ironically, the percentage of African Americans in the population was higher. The subsistence needs of the poor were attended by the biracial political alliance that Mayor Scott and Councilor Brown forged. This regime was tolerated by the seafood packers who had no interest whatsoever in economic development.

Had Scotty and Brown attempted to implement programs that threatened to bring about far-reaching social, economic, or political change, it seems likely that the packers or the county elites would have tried to stop them. Ambitious programs were out of the question, however, because of Crisfield's near total dearth of resources. Furthermore, a subsistence regime is conservative in the sense that it is resistent to most forms of change, which burden the poor. In spite of their relatively few years of schooling, many Crisfield residents seemed as cognizant as Polanyi was of the destructive effects that market forces could have on the social fabric of their small city. Because Crisfield was a miniature social democracy, its working-class citizens dreaded the prospect of being displaced and absorbed into the more hierarchical social and political order that prevailed in the Princess Anne region.

DISCUSSION

The cases of Princess Anne and Crisfield support a number of propositions that have applicability and significance beyond these immediate objects of study. First, granting that individuals were rational in the way they pursued their preferences, this rationality differed from the neoclassical concept of 'economic man.' Preferences could not be reduced to simple calculations of loss or gain. In fact, both case studies illustrate that the way individuals perceive their interests and develop their policy preferences is highly contingent upon the social and historical context of their lives. The logic of their situation can vary from time to time and from place to place, depending upon historically given circumstances, the prevailing way of life in a given community, and the individual's place in the social order.

It is evident that, in Somerset County, economic growth can be threatening to both "haves" and "have nots." The planters, in an earlier period, and the packers still have a stake in maintaining a pool of cheap surplus labor, which, presumably, would dwindle if economic development fulfilled its promise to bring in jobs. But it is not only the monopolistic interests of elites that growth can endanger. Small business failures tend to increase when taxes and wages rise. The notorious case of Atlantic City, New Jersey, also bears witness to the fact that disadvantaged groups can be pushed aside when growth occurs.[4] We may conclude that while top down economic development that is fostered by business elites with land interests may produce growth in the long run, it may also impose sociocultural and material harms upon vulnerable groups, and in some communities that might mean the majority.

These case studies show that preferences may be nonmaterial as well as material in nature. The watermen have fought to protect their independence, their equal status, and their unique way of life on the water. They have wanted to protect themselves and their children from being shamed and displaced by outsiders with more education, outside contacts, and money.

Power per se has enough appeal that elites and others wanted to hold on to whatever amount they possess. We have seen that the jealous guarding of power created mistrust across sectors. When Crisfield responded to the crisis of three plant closings, and the chamber apparently could not bring itself to open the supposedly communitywide Business Forum to seafood people and blacks, the result was that a rare opportunity to unite the community behind an economic revitalization plan was lost. Privilege had taken precedence over the community's interest.

Quality of life was the overriding preference for many newcomers who chose to live in Princess Anne or Crisfield because of the quaintness, charm, and small-town amenities they offered.

Many of these were older people and retirees who were not seeking to maximize their economic gain but to find a modicum of security on a fixed income, and growth was a threat to their values too.

The variety of preferences among individuals in these two communities, and the dramatically different economic development policies they adopted, lend support to Granovetter's argument that purposive action is always "embedded in ongoing systems of social relations."[5] Additionally, this work argues that all social structures are complex combinations of Gemeinschaft and Gesellschaft and that dualistic thinking has obscured this important fact and its policy ramifications. Social and political hierarchy and affective relations are always at stake in economic development policy. One obvious implication is that scholars should examine large cities to see how cultural values influence economic policy making.

Further contradicting the market model, there was little evidence in either town of a unitary view of economic progress. Each segment of the population nurtured its own view of the kind of development that should be fostered. For example, the EDC took the position that the community was too poor to be selective about the kind of industry or growth it attracted.[6] Under its auspices, the state prison and the foul clam plant were recruited. But, the citizens' group People United (P.U.!) agreed with state planners that Princess Anne should be promoted to tourists and retirees as a historical showplace. Obviously, these two visions of growth were in complete opposition. Although city planning documents existed, and new ones were regularly produced, planned development had few active proponents in Somerset County. This state of affairs can be attributed to the preoccupation of elites with protecting their privilege.

Finally, these case studies demonstrate that if cultures can be evaluated by the extent to which they value and safeguard the dignity and worth of the individual, independent of his or her social or material status, then working-class cultures of the kind found in Crisfield may be just as worthy of protection as middle-class cultures, and neither they nor the people who cling to them should be viewed as expendable, which has happened too often.[7]

IMPLICATIONS

Clientelism

When Somerset County's traditional way of life is examined in detail, it reveals a system for regulating the flow of resources that is rooted in the social class structure and closely parallels patron-client relations.[8] Clientelism is based upon highly asymmetrical but mutually dependent relationships between employer and employee or client and patron. In other words, "elite and privileged classes develop ties of mutual obligation with the poor and the powerless by acting as patrons who facilitate access to scarce material and social resources."[9]

While clientelism is typical of the way that power relationships are structured in Third World democracies, this phenomenon is not limited to developing nations. Newby and his colleagues documented the existence of comparable structures in England's rural Suffolk County,[10] and scholars have likewise compared U.S. urban political machines with clientelistic forms.[11] What is clear, then, is that, while Somerset's particular combination of social structures and culture has unique aspects, it is neither an isolated curiosity, nor an atavistic throwback to a previous era, nor even an exclusively rural phenomenon. It is a distinctive system for regulating power relations and exchange that is widespread throughout the developed and undeveloped world in human settlements of all sizes.

When Gaventa found social structures in a coal mining community in Appalachia that constituted, in this view, another manifestation of clientelism, he noted that if the processes of power that he found operating there were more general in source, "then they may be similar in nature and consequence for rural or urban, subculture or mainstream, black or white relatively powerless people everywhere."[12]

The words of an analyst of Jamaican society confirm the theoretical importance of clientelistic structures:

These factors that constitute the clientelistic system of democracy are not mere points of deviation from the metropolitan model of pluralist or liberal democracy. They represent a logical system of power, competition for power, values, norms, bases of affiliation, and patterns of political participation that amount to a well-defined political culture that is understood by the political actors in the system but defies classification by the existing concepts, paradigms and theories governing competitive party politics and electoral democracy.[13]

Considering clientelism's frequent appearance in places where poverty is entrenched and inequalities are extreme, its existence should be expected wherever conditions of this kind prevail.

Somerset County's clientelistic social structures grew out of an impoverished community that was characterized by the extreme inequality of access to power, capital, and economic and social opportunity that is typical of former slave societies. The vertical relationships between landlords and tenants, for example, or seafood packers and pickers, were informal, personalized, and highly particularistic. They were cemented by ties of loyalty and mutual obligation that rendered the organized expression of discontent highly unlikely.[14] And, as in the English case, political issues were individualized, which further reduced the likelihood of mobilization for collective political action.

Clientelistic social structures naturally give rise to what Bachrach and Baratz have called the "second face of power," which manifests itself in nondecision making.[15] This means that the expression of political opposition is held in check by the problem of anticipated reactions. Potential opponents tend to remain silent on sensitive policy issues because of their wish to avoid repercussions, thus leaving elites in control of the policy agenda. Newby and his colleagues found, for example, that in Suffolk, "where the same individuals dominate the political system, the employment market, the distribution of local public housing, the local legal institutions such as the magistracy, and are still sources of local welfare and patronage, there is likely to be a strong disincentive for less powerful and more dependent groups to mount a challenge against them."[16]

The second face of power was evident in Somerset also. Opposition to the planter's regime was weak, and the expression of dissent was muted, because people were reluctant to voice their opinions if they were personally vulnerable to powerful patrons. The modus operandi of the governing group was to co-opt independent interests and discourage the expression of policy concerns that conflicted with their agenda.

In the past, the ruling group had sometimes acted outside of the law, as, for example, in the case of the Princess Anne lynching and its subsequent cover-up. In the present, any criticism or questioning of the actions of those in power continued to be received as a personal challenge. Therefore, other groups were unlikely to express their dissenting views because of the anticipated reactions of those on whom they depended for access to life's essentials, such as jobs, credit, housing, and so forth. Gaventa observes that "participation denied over time may lead to acceptance of the role of non-participation, as well as to a failure to develop the political resources—skills, organization, consciousness—of political action."[17] This was also the case in Somerset County, where highly personalized power relations had, over time, fostered a view of public office and public authority as the private preserve of traditional elites. Thus it came as a rude shock to the governing group in Princess Anne when insurgents won four out of five seats on the town commission.

The consequences of violating taboos against political insurgency and breaches of white caste loyalty should not be minimized. The quickness with which the good ole boys acted to reassert their dominance in the aftermath of the upset election served as a public warning to the community of outsiders and blacks that had led the electoral uprising. While the use of extra-legal violence seemed to have become a thing of the past, the insurgents in Princess Anne were nonetheless subjected to threats and harassment that were disturbing enough to induce some of the newly elected officials to step down.

The power of the racial caste system and other countywide structural and cultural features to shape individual preferences and patterns of behavior can be understood, in part, in terms of the universal human needs for trust, predictability, and economy of action. The social acceptance that conformity insured provided individuals with important dimensions of personal security and perhaps even safety. In the context of this Southern black belt culture, where there was a lingering perception of the ruling group as being capable of resorting to ruthless and possibly illegal measures to enforce its dominance, it was the rare individual who could stand apart from his or her social milieu and critically evaluate the assumptions that guided thought and behavior.

Although this research could neither confirm nor disprove it, confidential informant interviews uncovered widespread beliefs about elite misuse of the criminal-justice system to harass and punish both blacks and whites who dared to challenge the formal and informal authority structures. Regardless of whether these scenarios were real or imagined, it is certain that many people believed they were real, and the belief itself had a strong inhibitory effect. Thus we see that the pressure to participate uncritically in the cultural mindset was not based upon psychological needs only. There were perceived material consequences for blacks and whites alike who challenged or otherwise defied established political and racial norms. Even though overt repression, or coercion, was not ascertainably a part of the repertoire of contemporary elites, control of social and material inducements was enough in itself to endow them with significant power, which was augmented by the special vulnerability of the population. Merely to secure a subsistence was an overriding goal for most of the county's poor.

Subsistence Cultures

"Modernization operates like a giant steel hammer, smashing both traditional institutions and traditional structures of meaning. It deprives the individual of the security which . . . traditional institutions provided for him," according to one scholar.[18] This is because, in traditional societies, the subsistence needs of an economically vulnerable people typically have led to the formation of informal exchange structures and cultural values that often conflict with market mores. Call this the "values theory" of preference formation.

The top-down economic development that was attempted in Princess Anne and that the inner chamber tried to bring to Crisfield is appealing to educated groups that are rich in resources and skillful in exploiting growth opportunities. But it violates the less instrumental values of others for whom subsistence concerns take priority over profitability. Mayor Scott gave expression to those values when he refused to authorize the eviction of Reverend Best from the Arcade Theatre in Crisfield, saying that there had to be a better way to handle the problem of the nonpaying tenant than putting him out in the cold.

This study found that economic development, as it is conventionally conceived and practiced, is based upon neoclassical assumptions of economic rationality that had no general applicability to the residents of Somerset County. There were institutions in place in the black community and among the watermen and others that functioned to insure that the subsistence needs of each member of the community would be met, albeit minimally. And these institutions imbued the culture with values and meanings that were markedly different from those of "economic man."

In his discussion of subsistence cultures in Southeast Asia, Scott urges us not to treat the peasant "purely as a kind of marketplace individualist who amorally ransacks his environment so as to reach his personal goal—that is, the stabilization of his subsistence arrangements." For to do so is to miss

> the central fact that the peasant is born into a society and culture that provide him with a fund of moral values, a set of concrete social relationships, a pattern of expectations about the behavior of others, and a sense of how those in his culture have proceeded to similar goals in the past. . . . To say that people are born into society is not to deny their capacity to create new forms and break old ones; it is merely to recall that they do not walk out on an empty stage and make up their lines at random."[19]

Subsistence cultures are labeled differently by the scholars who study them; for example, Scott refers to the "moral economy" of peasants in Southeast Asia, and Goren Hyden writes about "economies of affection" in communities throughout Africa. What all of these studies have in common is that they describe informal exchange structures, based upon trust, that are maintained by strong norms of reciprocity and mutual obligation that extend to all members of the community, however the community is defined, and they function to preserve a particular moral order and to minimize and spread risk.[20] Hyden observed that they have a welfare function for the poor that formal institutions cannot match.[21]

This work demonstrates that economic development poses a threat to the interests of individuals who are without extra material resources. Vidich and Bensmen reported a "psychology of scarcity" among small businessmen operating near the margin. Fearful of risk, they favored low-tax and low-government expenditure policies.[22] Other scholars have detailed the economic costs and burdens that growth, rationalization, and efficiency impose upon vulnerable groups.[23] Market forces can also wreak destruction upon the traditional institutions and values that provide a modicum of security for the poor.

While the "power theory" and the "values theory" may seem at first glance to offer alternative or conflicting explanations for the resistence to economic development among Somerset's poor people, these theories are in fact complementary. When James Scott noted that risk avoidance is the guiding principal in the culture wherever subsistence economies prevail, he referred to economic risk,[24] but we have seen that in Somerset County political and economic risk were inseparable. Recall that major economic change disrupts power relations, degrades cultural values, and upsets delicately balanced subsistance arrangements. Those who lived close to the margin were thus trapped in a political and economic doublebind. For the poor, to embrace uncontrolled economic development would have meant jeopardizing their subsistence arrangements, abjuring their dependence upon powerful patrons, and betraying deeply internalized community values that their social status and personal security depended upon—all on the remote chance that they personally would profit from development policies that held out hope for improved economic opportunities only in the long run and that were speculative at best. Like Logan and Molotch, many of Somerset's poor people believed that the land speculators, developers, and rentiers would prove to be the real beneficiaries of economic development in the end.[25] These concerns should prompt us to completely rethink top-down approaches to economic development policy.

Inequality and Inefficiency

There is a loss of social intelligence when high resource groups can secure a privileged position and shape the regime on their terms by parceling out contingent privileges and necessities.[26] This is because elites who are able to discipline others to go along with their preferred agenda have little incentive to offer forums to outsider groups. Moreover, "the greater the privilege being protected, the less the incentive to understand and act on behalf of the community in its entirety."[27]

Under these conditions, a wide range of policy options may not be considered. Indeed, they may never be articulated at all because of a fear of anticipated reactions. Furthermore, the policies that are enacted may have deleterious consequences, not only for those segments of the community that were unable to voice their opposition during the policy formation process, but for the community as a whole.

As an illustration of how clientelistic social structures have limited the problem-solving capacity of local government in Somerset County and led to ineffective responses to economic decline, consider again the racial caste system and the related practice of co-opting black leaders who then served to keep other blacks in line. These were structures that defined opportunities and limits for African Americans, and they engendered a mindset that was characterized by fear and resentment of whites and vigilant guarding against any word or action that might bring renewed repression upon the black community. The suppression of public discourse about economic and other issues of concern to working class blacks was one of many effects of this social practice.

Another effect was the reinforcing of bigotry in the white population. The resulting disregard for the aspirations of the black community had further implications for economic-development policy, especially when the interests of haves and have-nots conflicted. In a county where white planters and seafood packers had long associated their interests with maintaining a large supply of cheap labor, the ruling group did not scruple to limit employment opportunities for the black labor force. In the past, the planter's regime had also limited educational opportunities for African Americans in order to ensure the continuing dependence of the work force and ward off development. The ongoing legacy of a severely undereducated population has sharply restricted the county's development options up to the present.

Protection of privilege diminished the governing group's willingness to consider a wide range of policy options and also its capacity to view local issues in terms of an overarching community interest. The risk in this situation, according to urban regime theorist Clarence N. Stone, is that decision makers, by excluding affected groups from meaningful participation in the policymaking process, have an inadequate grasp of the consequences of their actions.

A genuinely effective regime is able to comprehend the consequences of its actions for a diverse citizenry. Democracy has to operate with a commitment to inclusiveness. Permanent or excluded minorities are inconsistent with the basic idea of equality that underpins democracy. This is why some notion of social learning is an essential part of the democratic process: all are entitled to have their situations understood. Thus to the extent that urban regimes safeguard special privilege at the expense of social learning, democracy is weakened.[28]

It does not seem farfetched to conclude that Somerset's seemingly permanent status as Maryland's poorest county can be attributed at least in part to its clientelistic social structures that have not only prompted the exclusion of major segments of society from any meaningful form of political participation beyond the franchise, but have also ruled out serious and sustained attention by decisionmakers to the welfare of most of the county's residents.

Economic and Political Disequilibrium

These two case studies have implications regarding how economic change ramifies at the local level—a subject on which economics and political science sometimes disagree. Theodore Schultz points out in *Restoring Economic Equilibrium* that the disequalibria resulting from economic change are omitted from the core of much economic theory. This is because the dominant strain in economic theory—and political theories that are derived from it—depends upon "a tendency assumption" that is "based on the proposition that there is . . . a tendency toward equilibrium, and that it suffices."[29] Because the assumed tendency toward equilibrium is judged thus to suffice, these theories logically need not address the important questions of how the human agent acts to bring her or his economic domain into equilibrium in the aftermath of disequilibrating economic change induced by acts of nature, public policy, market growth, decline, or other causes, and what the social and political consequences of those activities might be.

Regime theory is less reticent, however, about who gets what, when, and why, when economic change occurs. Change is inevitable, in this view, and conflict is to be expected as political actors struggle over what the terms of the change are to be. The regime analysis presented here is consistent with Schultz's critique of economic-development policies and growth models in that it demonstrates the conceptual inadequacy of mainstream economic theory's assumption of an equilibrium tendency. In concrete, historical detail, it reports actions taken by human agents to establish or restore equilibrium in their private domains in response to disturbances caused by serious, prolonged economic decline. These case studies illustrate a kind of economic action on which the core of neoclassical economics and political theories that are derived from it are virtually silent. Moreover, the case of Princess Anne demonstrates once again—for it is not a new idea—that profoundly disequilibrating economic change can prompt human agents to take actions that eventuate in political as well as economic restructuring.[30] Major economic change, either growth or decline, should be viewed as a politically as well as economically disequilibrating event.

CONCLUSION

Since economic reductionism cannot explain the variety of responses to market forces that can readily be observed in different communities, my hope is that this research has contributed not only to an understanding of how individual preferences are formed, but also to a grasp of the intricate mechanisms by which the preferences of some groups, rather than others, become public policy.

Also important are the lessons that Princess Anne and Crisfield can teach about economic development. We have seen that market calculations of impacts of development projects that fail to take account of nonmarket values are susceptible to the error of overestimating their benefits and underestimating their real costs. Unless market forces are carefully harnessed to some equitable conception of the community's interest that goes beyond an aggregation of the presumed mercenary motives of atomistic individuals, economic growth is likely to do at least as much harm as good and perhaps far more. As Councilor Milbourne explained to the Crisfield Area Chamber of Commerce, there are values and concerns in local communities that are not commercial, and those who would govern should, in all justice, be made to sleep with the consequences of their policy decisions.[31]

These cases suggest that there is a need for new theories to replace the currently fashionable economic explanations of local development policy. They further imply that policy prescriptions that are based upon deductive inferences about people's interests are per se flawed, because they fail to take singular local history and way-of-life factors into account. By extending regime theory to include the formative influence of social structures and culture in local communities, the present work offers an empirically grounded alternative to the market model that is applicable to communities of all sizes.

The causal argument advanced in this book is that individuals pursue their preferences within the context of particular institutions, cultures, and historically given circumstances, and that their actions, being shaped by these contextual variables, convey influence from structural antecedent to structural consequent. Thus the explanations presented here are consistent with methodological individualism, because the causal structures and the mechanisms of change (or pattern maintenance) are grounded in individual agency.[32] The lack of great social complexity in Princess Anne and Crisfield allows the relationship between structure and agency—and the mechanisms by which each exerts influence—to stand out with unusual clarity.

Indeed, one of the most interesting results of these case studies is the extent to which they reveal that agency matters. Actors made judgments and policy decisions within a social context, to be sure, and the evidence attests that they were powerfully influenced by contextual variables. That is the central thesis of this book. But as their stories unfolded, it became clear that individuals often wrestled with conflicting impulses and conflicting values before making policy choices.

Sometimes political actors agonized over questions such as whom to trust and what to believe when choosing between alternative policy options. This was an especially acute dilemma for black leaders, at times, in deciding which white faction to support or align with. Recall that Roland Brown first supported an urban renewal slum clearance project and later repented of it, feeling that he and the black community that he represented had been badly betrayed. And when faced with complex moral dilemmas, such as whether or not to risk challenging established authority for the sake of a greater good, individuals often engaged in internal struggles between self-serving instincts and consciences that were attuned to a higher authority.

Therefore, one of the most powerful lessons to be drawn from the experience of Princess Anne and Crisfield is that regardless of how fervently human beings may wish to deny their moral autonomy in order to escape from the burdens that individual responsibility imposes, ultimately, there is no such "escape from freedom."[33] Under the pressures of national and global forces and local institutional tendencies, individuals in these communities sometimes chose well and sometimes chose badly. Still, they chose.

Notes

Preface

1. A scholar who read part of my work asked how I could rely so heavily upon the Princess Anne newspaper when I have, in effect, stated that it was unreliable. Amidst the editorializing and selective reporting, the *Somerset Herald*, like any newspaper, reported a great many facts. My task was to analyze and interpret those facts. I noticed, for example, that every time the name Tony Bruce—a lawyer and key figure in local politics—was mentioned, the *Herald* reported one of his institutional affiliations or the names of clients that he represented. But Bruce's affiliations were never reported in one place. Neither was that information available to me from other sources. I therefore started a special "Tony Bruce" file on my word processor, and every time the newspapers reported one of his affiliations, I entered it. In this way, the extensive interlocking networks and directorates that this civic notable was almost invariably at the center of gradually emerged into view. I was able to make the county's "hidden government" visible through this and other devices.

2. These were Paul Peterson's market model of economic development policy, John Logan and Harvey Molotch's growth machine thesis, and urban regime theory as developed by Steve Elkin, Clarence N. Stone, Todd Swanstrom, and others.

3. Freire (1993); Shor and Freire (1987); and Shor (1987, 1992).

4. Paolo Freire in Shor and Freire (1987:56).

5. See Shor and Freire (1987); and Sternberg (1981).

6. At least, I feel sure that it would not surprise Jean Jacques Rousseau, Mary Wollstonecraft, J. S. Mill, Carole Pateman, or Bachrach and

Botwinick, all of whom have viewed small scale participatory democracy as a prime mechanism for human moral development.

7. See Watzlawick's (1978) explanation of the *pars-pro-toto* principle and other mental processes involved in intellectual synthesis.

8. See Monti (1990:xx).

CHAPTER 1

1. Ellis (1986:2) presents an interesting sociological study of how "these maritime backwater peninsulas and out-of-the-way islands" dealt with impinging forces for social change in the two decades preceding the present study.

2. Wennersten (unpublished:24).

3. Wennersten (1992).

4. Callcott (1985:11).

5. Between 1980 and 1990, the town of Princess Anne witnessed a loss of white population, which was more than offset by an increase in the number of blacks. The total population in the town thus increased from 1,499 to 1,666, with the proportion of blacks rising from 48 to 51 percent. Crisfield also witnessed a loss of white population, but this was not offset by the city's small increase in the number of blacks. Hence Crisfield's total population fell from 2,924 to 2,880, and the black population increased from 32 to 35 percent.

6. Somerset County's per capita income was about 64 percent of the statewide average in 1987. Its twenty-four-month average unemployment rate of 10.1 percent was more than double the statewide average of 4.7 percent for the same period ending in 1988. The county's five-year unemployment average for the period between 1982 and 1988 was 9.9 percent, while the state's average during the same period was 4.4 percent. In February 1989, the county's unemployment figure of 12.9 percent was triple the statewide average of 4.2 percent (UMES, 1989).

7. Falk and Zhou (1989); Picou, Wells, and Nyberg (1978); Sokolow (1981); Summers (1986); Swanson et al. (1979).

8. Peterson (1981).

9. Ibid.

10. Finsterbusch (1992).

11. Staniland (1985).

12. Granovetter (1985).

13. Ibid.; Logan and Swanstrom (1990); Polanyi (1957); Portes and Sensenbrenner (1993); Staniland (1985); and Swanstrom (1993).

14. Little (1989).

15. Stinchcombe (1968).

16. See Stone (1989).

17. Abrams (1982:2).

18. I use Little's (1989) term *instigating events* interchangeably with *potentially restructuring events.*

19. Goulet (1973:326).

20. Ibid.

21. I am indebted to Denis Goulet for suggesting this metaphor.

CHAPTER 2

1. Bluestone and Harrison (1982); Falk and Lyson (1988).

2. Peterson (1981).

3. Fainstein et al. (1983); Logan and Molotch (1987); Logan and Swanstrom (1990); Mollenkopf (1983); Molotch (1976, 1993); Smith (1984); Stone and Sanders (1987); Stone (1989, 1993); Swanstrom (1985); Whitt (1982).

4. Polanyi (1957).

5. Staniland (1985:49).

6. While it has been useful in some cases to explain the causes of rural poverty and underdevelopment in the United States in terms of third world development theories (e.g., Billings 1979; Davidson 1990; Gaventa et al. 1990), the social embeddedness argument shows that there are difficulties with using global theories that fail to take local institutions, history, and culture into account when explaining local political responses to market force (Staniland, 1985; Swanstrom 1993).

7. Hunter (1953).

8. Ibid.; Dahl (1961); Banfield and Wilson (1963); Wolfinger (1974).

9. See also Domhoff (1978), Harvey (1973), and Polsby (1980).

10. Elkin (1987), Stone (1987, 1989), and Swanstrom (1985) are the main architects of urban-regime theory.

11. See Stone (1994) and Swanstrom (1985).

12. Elkin (1987).

13. Stone (1987, 1989, 1993).

14. DeLeon (1992).

15. Swanstrom (1991:42). Swanstrom's (1985) *The Crisis of Growth Politics* made a seminal contribution in the development of this paradigm.

16. Peterson (1981:38).

17. Ibid. (1981:149).

18. Ibid. (129).

19. Ibid. (12).

20. Ibid. (32).

21. Ibid. (149).

22. See USDA (1987).

23. Swanstrom (1991:44).

24. Logan and Molotch (1987).

25. Ibid. (32).

26. Ibid. (71).

27. Molotch (1976:314).

28. Ibid. (1976:310).

29. Logan and Molotch (1987).

30. Ibid. (1987:98).

31. Stone (1989).

32. Swanstrom (1988).

33. See Eisenstadt and Shachar (1987).

34. Wirth (1938).

35. Ibid.

36. Bender (1978:16).

37. Ibid:25

38. Bender (1978:26).

39. Ibid.

40. Bender (1978: 31–43).

41. Gans (1991:23)

42. Wilson (1993:710).

43. Espiritu and Light (1991:45).

44. Ibid: (50).

45. Portes and Rumbaut (1990); Zhou (1992).

46. Portes and Sensenbrenner (1993).

47. Eckstein (1988); Wildavsky (1987).

48. Rosdil (1991:79).

49. Long (1991).

50. Long (1983).

51. Ibid: (41).

52. Ibid: (23).

53. Ibid: (29).

54. Ibid: (21).

55. Warner (1968).

56. Long (1983:41).

57. Ibid: (24).

58. Long (1991:6).

59. Swanstrom (1988:108–109). Stone (1987) identifies corporate, progressive, and caretaker regimes.

60. Molotch (1993).

CHAPTER 3

1. Key (1949:554).

2. Maryland Department of State Planning (1990).

3. Carr (1988).

4. Warner (1987).

5. Lawson (1988).

6. Warner (1987).

7. Before being renamed by a Methodist minister, Dames Quarter was Damned Quarter, Deal's Island was Devil's Island, Rhodes Point was Rogue's Point. Crisfield was originally known as Ape's Hole.

8. According to Ellis (1986), the "church was the central institution of the Island. Serving as the actual polity, it organized other institutions and provided resources for health care, recreation, utilities such as street lighting, family assistance, and other needs of the community. All social activity was sponsored though the church. All clubs and volunteer organizations such as the Fireman's Association, PTA, and Boy Scouts functioned through the church. Whenever something needed to be done in the community, such as installing a sewer or paving roads, it was brought up in church and a church committee was formed for that purpose. The Island nurse (a church employee) said, 'If ever I need anything for the Medical Center, I just stand up at a church meeting and ask for it and pretty soon it is taken care of.' . . . The Council of Ministries served as the town council. . . . The minister acted as de facto mayor of the island" (66–67).

9. Historian John Wennersten reports that so great was the resentment against free blacks by white inhabitants, because they were needed as laborers, and, perhaps more important, because some were more prosperous than whites, that the Somerset County delegation to the Maryland General Assembly attempted, unsuccessfully, to have them legally enslaved.

10. In 1990, Princess Anne's population was 51 percent black and Crisfield's population was 35 percent black, according to the census.

11. Brugger (1988); Kulikoff (1986).

12. Kulikoff (1986:5).

13. Ibid.

14. Cited in Hoffman (1973).

15. Especially the property requirements for office holders and the system of public voting by voice, "which served to intimidate an overly independent voter" (Ridgway, 1979:5).

16. Wennersten (1981:8).

17. Ibid.

18. Callcott (1985), Ridgway (1979).

19. Kulikoff (1986:43).

20. Ridgeway (1979).

21. Wennersten (1981:12).

22. Ibid. (11).

23. Callcott (1975:9).

24. Ibid.

25. Ibid.

26. Ibid. (25).

27. Black and Black (1987).

28. Brugger (1988:309).

29. See V. O. Key, Jr. (1949) for the classic treatise on the post-Reconstruction disfranchisement drive against Southern blacks and the simultaneous creation of the Democratic "solid South."

30. Callcott (1975).

31. Reed and Singel (1982).

32. Callcott (1975). See also Kousser (1974).

33. Callcott (1975: 225).

34. Key (1949).

35. Cash (1941).

36. See Reed (1986) on violence as a component of Southern culture.

37. Three counties constitute the Lower Eastern Shore: Somerset, Wicomico, and Worcester.

38. Wennersten (unpublished: p 232).

39. Brugger (1988).

40. Raper (1933:41–42).

41. Mencken (1931).

42. Callcott (1985:101); Brugger (1988:508).

43. Ibid.

44. Raper (1933).

45. Cash (1941).

46. According to Wennersten (unpublished), "Between 1889 and 1930, 3,724 people were lynched in the South; over 4/5 of these were blacks. In practically every case no determined effort for the conviction of the lynchers was made in a community where a lynching occurred . . . during the period 1929–1932, forty-five blacks were murdered." (347–48)

47. James (1988) refers to this phenomenon in the South as the "racial state," arguing that local states are strongly constrained by local class structures, and also provide opportunities for oligarchs.

48. See Callcott's chapter "The Four Cultures of Maryland" (1985:1–28).

49. Callcott (1985:146).

50. Ibid.

51. Ibid. (146).

52. Ibid.

53. Ibid. (149–50).

54. Ibid. (151–52).

55. Ibid. (152).

56. See Callcott (1985) for a full account of Maryland's outstanding record in achieving integration, as well as civil rights legislation, during this period.

57. Wennersten (unpublished).

58. Quoted in ibid.

59. Wennersten (unpublished).

60. Callcott (1985).

61. Wennersten (unpublished).

62. Ibid.

63. Ibid.

64. Somerset County School Board meeting with NAACP Education Committee on June 18, 1991.

65. A confidential informant.

66. Overheard in a local restaurant.

67. Black and Black (1987); Genovese (1967); Key (1949).

68. See Billings (1988), Harrison (1985), Myrdal (1957), Raper (1933).

69. Mandle (1978).

70. Wiener (1978).

71. Wright (1986).

72. Carr (1988).

73. Raper (1933:41–42).

74. Dollard (1937). See also Myrdal (1957).

75. Myrdal (1962).

76. Reed (1986).

77. My research and cultural analysis were completed without reference to the work of James C. Scott. I first used the term *survival ethos* to describe the watermen's culture in a paper that I wrote for delivery at the Urban Affairs Association Meetings in Charlotte, NC, in 1990. At that time, I had not yet read Scott's (1976) *The Moral Economy of the Peasant*, in which he describes the "subsistence ethic" that is characteristic, he claims, of peasant society throughout the world. Scott includes fishing communities in his definition of peasant society. Thus the present work provides independent collaboration for many of Scott's claims.

78. Lawson (1988:20).

79. See Lawson (1988) and Warner (1987).

80. Warner (1987:89).

81. Ellis (1986).

82. Ibid.

83. Lawson (1988).

84. Callcott (1985).

85. Brugger (1988).

86. Ibid.; Lawson (1988).

87. Lawson (1988).

88. Warner (1976:72).

89. Lawson (1988).

90. Brugger (1988); Wennersten (1981).

91. Lawson (1988:110).

92. Ibid.

93. Ibid. (73).

94. Ibid. (101).

95. Ibid. (111).

96. Callcott (1985).

97. UMES (1989).

98. *Somerset Herald,* June 18, 1986.

99. Ibid.

100. Ibid., September 30, 1987.

101. Ibid., June 18, 1986.

102. Polanyi (1957:157).

103. Appallingly substandard conditions at the Westover Labor Camp, which is owned and operated by the Somerset Growers' Association, have been of ongoing concern to numerous organizations, agencies, and human rights advocacy groups for several decades. See "Migrant Workers on Maryland's Eastern Shore: A Report of the Maryland Advisory Committee to the United States Commission on Civil Rights" (June 1983).

104. Summers et al. (1988).

105. Gurr and King (1987).

106. UMES (1989).

107. See Browne (1982).

CHAPTER 4

1. This interpretation is based upon numerous interviews and informal conversations with county residents during a three year period. It is the same conclusion reached by Gibbons (1977) in *Wye Island: Outsiders, Insiders, and Resistance to Change.*

2. Finsterbusch et al. (1989).

3. See Gibbons (1977).

4. *Somerset Herald*, February 5, 1986.

5. Ibid., June 25, 1986.

6. Logan and Molotch (1987:29).

7. *Salisbury Daily Times*, September 28, 1990; *Somerset Herald*, November 8, 1989.

8. *Somerset Herald*, June 18, 1986.

9. Touart (1990).

10. *Somerset Herald*, June 22, 1988.

11. Ibid.

12. Ibid.

13. Ibid., July 5, 1989.

14. Ibid., August 9, 1989.

15. Ibid., December 21, 1988.

16. Ibid., July 12, 1989.

17. Ibid., August 23, 1989.

18. Ibid., August 9, 1989.

19. Ibid., September 6, 1989.

20. Ibid., September 27, 1989.

21. Callcott (1985).

22. *Somerset Herald*, September 9, 1989.

23. Ibid., October 4, 1989; November 15, 1989.

24. Ibid., March 14, 1990.

25. Ibid.

26. Ibid., March 21, 1990, to May 23, 1990.

27. Ibid., March 9, 1990.

28. Ibid., January 10, 1990.

29. Ibid., February 7, 1990.

30. Ibid., January 17, 1990.

31. Ibid., February 7, 1990.

32. Recorded March 23, 1990.

33. Ibid.

34. *Somerset Herald*, March 14, 1990.

35. Ibid., March 28, 1990.

36. Ibid., April 4, 1990.

37. Ibid., May 16, 1990.

38. Ibid.

39. It was reported that one of the reasons Hayward was recruited by the black community in Princess Anne to run for office was that he was employed in the Wicomico County school system and thus not vulnerable to manipulation by the superintendent of schools in Somerset County, who was viewed as a "system black."

40. Recorded June 18, 1990. See also *Salisbury Daily Times*, June 19, 1990.

41. Personal communication.

42. *Salisbury Daily Times*, September 16, 1991; *Somerset Herald*, September 12, 1991; September 26, 1990.

43. See for example *Somerset Herald*, July 18, 1990 to September 26, 1990.

44. Spoken in the author's presence in private conversation, and quoted with Shirley Richards's permission.

45. *Somerset Herald*, September 26, 1990; October 3, 1990.

46. Stone (1989:245).

47. *Somerset Herald*, October 3, 1990.

48. See Hanks (1987).

49. "There is going to be unrest until these people [blacks] can be made comfortable in their environment." This statement was offered as justification for the widespread development of trailer parks in Princess Anne. It is a telling expression of the paternalistic mindset.

50. *Salisbury Daily Times*, August 10, 1993.

51. See James's (1988) treatment of comparable phenomena in the southern United States.

52. Key (1949).

53. Kinnamon (1954).

54. Hanna (1907); Wallenstein (1987).

55. Callcott (1985).

56. See Schultz (1990); see also Baumgartner and Jones (1993).

CHAPTER 5

1. *Crisfield Times*, January 13, 1988, to May 1, 1991; *Somerset Herald*, January 20, 1988, to February 6, 1991.

2. Nondecision making refers to the power of elites to exercise some control over the policy agenda by preventing certain issues from being brought up for decision making (Bachrach and Baratz 1970).

3. A state official.

4. *Somerset Herald*, June 25, 1986.

5. Schumpeter (1950:250).

6. Callcott (1985:175).

7. *Crisfield Times*, January 2, 1991.

8. Stone (1989).

9. "Caretaker" typically refers to a regime based in a coalition of homeowners and small-property holders, whereas this text uses subsistence regime to describe policies based upon the subsistence requirements of a working class or peasant population living in or near poverty. The policy positions of the two regime types would, in most cases, be similar. See Stone and Sanders' (1987) on caretaker regimes.

10. *Crisfield Times*, August 30, 1989.

11. The "subsistence agenda," as the term is used here, is roughly equivalent to what Scott (1976) refers to as the "moral economy" of peasants in Southeast Asia.

12. See Reed (1987).

13. Stone (1989).

14. *Somerset Herald*, December 14, 1988.

15. Personal communication.

16. Wennersten (unpublished).

17. *Somerset Herald*, April 20, 1988.

18. Finsterbusch et al. (1990).

19. *Somerset Herald*, August 30, 1989.

20. A state employment official.

21. *Crisfield Times*, October 14, 1990.

22. The Crisfield Housing Authority.

23. See Bullard (1990) on the economic blackmail of poor rural communities.

24. *Somerset Herald*, May 15, 1985.

25. Ibid., July 20, 1988.

26. A city councilor.

27. *Somerset Herald*, June 10, 1992.

28. A state official.

29. *Crisfield Times*, February 14, 1990.

30. See Hanks (1987) for a discussion of a similar phenomenon, which he calls the "angel system," in three Georgia counties.

31. Source unknown.

32. A state official.

33. Scott (1976).

34. *Crisfield Times*, August 30, 1989.

35. *Somerset Herald*, August 6, 1989.

36. *Crisfield Times*, August 30, 1989.

37. Ibid., November 22, 1989.

38. Ibid.

39. Ibid.

40. From Wilson's letter to Jay Tawes, November 5, 1990.

41. Granovetter (1985:487).

42. Logan and Molotch (1987).

43. Polanyi (1957).

44. See Billings (1979).

45. Ellis (1986); Lawson (1988).

46. See Scott's (1976) discussion of the "subsistence ethic" and Vidich and Bensmen (1960) for their important concept of the 'mentality of scarcity.'

47. Scholars have reported similar patterns of personalized political responses in rural England (Newby, et al. 1979).

CHAPTER 6

1. Callcott (1985).

2. Stone (1988:19).

3. Cash (1941:223).

4. Sternlieb and Hughes (1983).

5. Granovetter (1985).

6. Address presented by Thomas Laidlaw, executive director of the Economic Development Commission of Somerset County, at the annual meeting of the Community Resource Development Association, June 1991, University of Maryland Eastern Shore.

7. I am grateful to Norton E. Long for pointing out this implication of the findings.

8. See Eisenstadt and Roniger (1984).

9. Stone, Carl (1980:96–97).

10. Newby et al. (1979:130).

11. See Schmidt et al. (1977). Cf. Erie (1988).

12. Gaventa (1980:260).

13. Stone, Carl (1980:108–9).

14. See Eisenstadt and Roniger (1984).

15. Bachrach and Baratz (1970).

16. Newby et al. (1979:130).

17. Gaventa (1980:255).

18. Berger (1976:23).

19. Scott (1976:166).

20. See Booth's (1994) insightful analysis of the idea of a moral economy, published as this book goes to press.

21. Hyden (1983).

22. Vidich and Bensmen (1960).

23. Feagin and Parker (1990); Holli (1969).

24. Scott (1976).

25. Logan and Molotch (1987).

26. Stone (1992:63).

27. Ibid.

28. Ibid. (63).

29. Schultz (1990).

30. Fainstein (1990); Mollenkopf (1992).

31. See chapter 5.

32. See Little (1989:220).

33. Fromm (1941).

Abrams, Philip. 1982. *Historical Sociology*. Ithaca, New York: Cornell University Press.

Bachrach, Peter, and Morton S. Baratz. 1970. *Power and Poverty*. New York: Oxford University Press.

Banfield, Edward C., and James Q. Wilson. 1963. *City Politics*. Cambridge, MA: Harvard University Press.

Baumgartner, Frank R., and Bryan D. Jones. 1993. *Agendas and Instability in American Politics*. Chicago: The University of Chicago Press.

Beaulieu, Lionel J., ed. 1988. *The Rural South in Crisis: Challenges for the Future*. Boulder: Westview Press.

Bender, Thomas. 1978. *Community and Social Change in America*. New Brunswick: Rutgers University Press.

Berger, Peter L. 1976. *Pyramids of Sacrifice: Political Ethics and Social Change*. Garden City: Anchor Books.

Billings, Dwight B., Jr. 1979. *Planters and the Making of a New South*. Chapel Hill: University of North Carolina Press.

———. "The Rural South in Crisis: A Historical Perspective." In *The Rural South in Crisis: Challenges for the Future*, ed. Lionel J. Beaulieu. Boulder: Westview Press.

Black, Earl, and Merle. 1987. *Politics and Society in the South*. Cambridge, MA: Harvard University Press.

Bluestone, Barry, and Bennett Harrison. 1982. *The Deindustrialization of America: Plant Closings, Community Abandonnment, and the Dismantling of Basic Industry.* New York: Basic Books.

Booth, William James. 1994. "On the Idea of a Moral Economy." *American Political Science Review* 88:653–67.

Browne, William P. 1982. "Political Values in a Changing Rural Community." In *Rural Policy Problems: Changing Dimensions*, ed. William P. Browne and D. F. Hadwiger. Lexington, MA: Lexington Books.

Brugger, Robert J. 1988. *Maryland: A Middle Temperament 1634–1980.* Baltimore: Johns Hopkins University Press.

Bullard, Robert D. 1987. "Blacks and the New South: Challenge of the Eighties." *Journal of Intergroup Relations* 15:25–39.

———. 1990. "Environmentalism, Economic Blackmail, and Civil Rights: Competing Agendas within the Black Community." In *Communities in Economic Crisis: Appalachia and the South*, ed. John Gaventa, Barbara Ellen Smith, and Alex Willingham. Philadelphia: Temple University Press.

Callcott, George H. 1985. *Maryland and America: 1940 to 1980.* Baltimore: Johns Hopkins University Press.

Callcott, Margaret L. 1975. *The Negro in Maryland Politics, 1870–1912.* Ann Arbor: Xerox University Microfilms.

Carr, Lois G., P. D. Morgan, and J. B. Russo, eds. 1988. *Colonial Chesapeake Society.* Chapel Hill: University of North Carolina Press.

Cash, Wilbur J. 1941. *The Mind of the South.* New York: Knopf.

Cobb, James C. 1982. *The Selling of the South.* Baton Rouge: Louisiana State University Press.

———. 1984. *Industrialization and Southern Society, 1877–1984.* Lexington: University of Kentucky Press.

Colclough, Glenna. 1988. "Uneven Development and Racial Composition in the Deep South: 1970–1980." *Rural Sociology* 53:73–86.

Crisfield Times. Crisfield, MD: Joni Silverstein, Publisher.

Dahl, Robert A. 1961. *Who Governs?* New Haven, CT: Yale University Press.

Davidson, Osha Gray. 1990. *Broken Heartland: The Rise of America's Rural Ghetto.* New York: Free Press.

DEED. 1989. Maryland Department of Economic and Employment Development. Office of Labor Market Analysis and Information. Baltimore, Maryland.

DeLeon, Richard Edward. 1992. *Left Coast City: Progressive Politics in San Francisco, 1975–1991*. Lawrence: University Press of Kansas.

Dewey, John. 1954. *The Public and Its Problems*. Denver, CO: Allan Swallow.

Dollard, John. 1937. *Caste and Class in a Southern Town*. 3d ed. Garden City: Doubleday.

Domhoff, G. William. 1978. *Who Really Rules: New Haven and Community Power Reexamined*. New Brunswick, NJ: Transaction.

Eckstein, Harry. 1988. "A Culturalist Theory of Political Change." *American Political Science Review*. 82:789–804.

Eisenstadt, S. N., and L. Roniger. 1984. *Patrons, Clients, and Friends: Interpersonal Relations and the Structure of Trust in Society*. Cambridge: University of Cambridge Press.

Eisenstadt, S. N., and A. Shachar. 1987. *Society, Culture, and Urbanization*. Newbury Park: Sage Publications.

Elkin, Stephen L. 1987. *City and Regime in the American Republic*. Chicago: University of Chicago Press.

Ellis, Carolyn. 1986. *Fisher Folk: Two Communities on Chesapeake Bay*. Lexington: University of Kentucky Press.

Erie, Steven P. 1988. *Rainbow's End: Irish–Americans and the Dilemmas of Urban Machine Politics, 1840–1985*. Berkeley and Los Angeles: University of California Press.

Espiritu, Yen Le, and Ivan Light. 1991. "The changing Ethnic Shape of Contemporary Urban America." In *Urban Life in Transition*, ed. M. Gottdeiner and Chris G. Pickvance. Newbury Park, CA: Sage Publications.

Fainstein, Susan S and Norman I. Fainstein. 1983. *Restructuring the City*. New York: Longman.

———. 1990. "Economics, Politics, and Development Policy." In *Beyond the City Limits*, ed. John R. Logan and Todd Swanstrom. Philadelphia: Temple University Press.

Falk, William W., and Thomas A. Lyson. 1988. *High Tech, Low Tech, No Tech: Recent Industrial and Occupational Change in the South.* Albany: State University of New York Press.

Falk, William W., and S. Zhao. 1989. "Paradigms, Theories, and Methods in Contemporary Rural Sociology: A Partial Replication and Extension." *Rural Sociology* 54:xx

Feagin, Joe R., and Robert Parker. 1990. *Building American Cities: The Urban Real Estate Game.* 2d ed. Englewood Cliffs, New Jersey: Prentice Hall.

Finsterbusch, Kurt, Cecelia Formicella, Daniel Kuennen, and Meredith Ramsay. 1990. "How Rural Counties Can Generate Jobs." *Sociological Practice* 8:167–82.

Finsterbusch, Kurt, Daniel Kuennen, and Meredith Ramsay. 1992. "An Evaluation of a Wide Range of Job–Generating Activities for Rural Counties." *Journal of the Community Development Society* 23:103–22.

Freire, Paulo. 1993. *Pedagogy of the Oppressed.* New York: Continuum.

Fromm, Erich. 1941. *Escape from Freedom.* New York: Rinehart and Winston.

Gans, Herbert J. 1962. *The Urban Villagers: Group and Class in the Life of Italian–Americans.* New York: Free Press.

———. 1991. *People, Plans, and Policies.* New York: Columbia University Press.

Gaventa, John. 1980. *Power and Powerlessness: Quiescence and Rebellion in an Appalachian Valley.* Urbana: University of Illinois Press.

Gaventa, John, and Helen Lewis. 1989. "Participatory Education and Grassroots Development: Current Experiences in Appalachia U.S.A." Paper presented at the annual meeting of the Southern Sociological Society, Norfolk, Virginia.

Gaventa, John, Barbara Ellen Smith, and Alex Willingham, eds. 1990. *Communities in Economic Crisis: Appalachia and the South.* Philadelphia: Temple University Press.

Genovese, Eugene D. 1967. *The Political Economy of Slavery.* New York: Vintage Books.

Gibbons, Boyd. 1977. *Wye Island: Outsiders, Insiders, and Resistance to Change.* Baltimore: Johns Hopkins University Press.

Goulet, Denis. 1973. *The Cruel Choice: A New Concept in the Theory of Development*. New York: Atheneum.

Granovetter, Mark. 1985. "Economic Action and Social Structure: The Problem of Embeddedness." *American Journal of Sociology* 91:481–510.

Green, Gary P., and Leann M. Tigges. 1989. "Economic Change in the Black Belt: Stages of Development or Underdevelopment?" Paper presented at the annual meeting of the Southern Sociological Society.

Gurr, Ted Robert, and Desmond S. King. 1987. *The State and the City*. London: Macmillan.

Hanks, Lawrence J. 1987. *The Struggle for Black Political Empowerment in Three Georgia Counties*. Knoxville: University of Tennessee Press.

Hanna, Hugh Sisson. 1907. *A Financial History of Maryland: 1789–1848*. Baltimore: Johns Hopkins University Press.

Harrison, Lawrence E. 1985. *Underdevelopment Is a State of Mind*. Lanham, MD: Madison Books.

Harvey, David. 1973. *Social Justice and the City*. Baltimore: Johns Hopkins University Press.

Hoffman, Ronald. 1973. *A Spirit of Dissension: Economics Politics, and the Revolution in Maryland*. Baltimore: Johns Hopkins University Press.

Holli, Melvin G. 1969. *Reform in Detroit*. New York: Oxford University Press.

Hunter, Floyd. 1953. *Community Power Structure*. Chapel Hill: University of North Carolina Press.

Hyden, Goran. 1983. *No Shortcuts to Progress: African Development Management in Perspective*. Berkeley and Los Angeles: University of California Press.

James, David R. 1988. "The Transformation of the Southern Racial State: Class and Race Determinants of Local–State Structures." *American Sociological Review* 53:191–208.

Key, V. O. Jr. 1949. *Southern Politics*. New York: Vintage Books.

Kinnamon, John A. 1954. *Internal Revenues of Colonial Maryland*. Springfield: University of Indiana Press.

148   References

Kousser, J. Morgan. 1974. *The Shaping of Southern Politics.* New Haven: Yale University Press.

Krannich, Richard S., and Craig R. Humphrey. 1983. "Local Mobilization and Community Growth: Toward an Assessment of the Growth Machine Hypothesis." *Rural Sociology* 48 (Spring):60–81.

Kulikoff, Allan. 1986. *Tobacco and Slaves: The Development of Southern Cultures in the Chesapeake 1680–1800.* Chapel Hill: University of North Carolina Press.

Lawson, Glenn. 1988. *The Last Waterman.* Crisfield, MD.: Crisfield Publishing Company.

Little, Daniel. 1989. *Understanding Peasant China: Case Studies in the Philosophy of Social Science.* New Haven: Yale University Press.

Logan, John R., and Harvey Molotch. 1987. *Urban Fortunes: The Political Economy of Place.* Berkeley: University of California Press.

Logan, John R. and Todd Swanstrom, eds. 1990. *Beyond the City Limits: Urban Policy and Economic Restructuring in Comparative Perspective.* Philadelphia: Temple University Press.

Long, Norton E. 1983. "Can the Contemporary City Be a Significant Polity?" Paper presented at the annual meeting of the Urban Affairs Association, March 23–26.

———. 1986. "The City as a Political Community." *Journal of Community Psychology* 14:72–80.

———. 1991. "The Paradox of a Community of Transients." *Urban Affairs Quarterly* 27:3–12.

Mandle, Jay. 1978. *The Roots of Black Poverty: The Southern Plantation Economy After the Civil War.* Durham: Duke University Press.

Maryland Advisory Committee to the United States Commission on Civil Rights. 1983. "Migrant Workers on Maryland's Eastern Shore."

Maryland Department of State Planning.

MDC, Inc. 1986. "Shadows in the Sunbelt: Developing the Rural South in an Era of Economic Change." A Report of the MDC Panel on Rural Economic Development.

Mencken, H. L. 1931. "The Eastern Shore Kultur." *The Baltimore Sun,* December 12, 1931.

Michie, Aruna Nayyar, ed. 1986. "Symposium on Rural Poverty and Public Policy in the United States." *Policy Studies Journal* 15 (December): 269–350.

Mollenkopf, John H. 1983. *The Contested City*. Princeton, NJ: Princeton University Press.

———. *A Phoenix in the Ashes*. Princeton, NJ: Princeton University Press.

Molotch, Harvey. 1976. "The City as a Growth Machine: Toward a Political Economy of Place." *American Journal of Sociology* 82, no. 2 (September): 309–32.

———. 1990. "Urban Deals in Comparative Perspective," in *Beyond the City Limits: Urban Policy and Economic Restructuring in Comparative Perspective*, eds. John R. Logan and Todd Swanstrom. Philadelphia: Temple University Press.

———. 1993. "The Political Economy of Growth Machines." *Journal of Urban Affairs*, 15:29–53.

Monti, Daniel J. 1990. *Race, Redevelopment, and the New Company Town*. Albany: State University of New York Press.

Myrdal, Gunner. 1957. *An American Dilemma: The Negro Problem and Modern Democracy*. New York: Harper and Brothers Publishers.

Newby, Howard, Peter Saunders, David Rose, and Collin Bell. 1979. "In Search of Community Power." In *Nonmetropolitan Industrial Growth and Community Change*, ed. Gene F. Summers and Anne Selvik. Lexington, MA: Lexington Books.

Peterson, Paul E. 1981. *City Limits*. Chicago: University of Chicago Press.

Picou, J. Steven, Richard H. Wells, and Kenneth L. Nyberg. 1978. "Paradigms, Theories and Methods in Contemporary Rural Sociology." *Rural Sociology* 43 (Winter): 559–83.

Polanyi, Karl. 1957. *The Great Transformation: The Political and Economic Origins of Our Time*. Boston: Beacon Press.

Polsby, Nelson W. 1980. *Community Power and Community Theory: A Further Look at Problems of Evidence and Inference*. New Haven: Yale University Press.

Portes, Alejandro, and R. G. Rumbaut. 1990. *Immigrant America: A Portrait*. Berkeley and Los Angeles: University of California Press.

Portes, Alejandro, and Julia Sensenbrenner. "Embeddedness and Immigration: Notes on the Social Determinants of Economic Action." *American Journal of Sociology*, 98, no. 6 (May 1993):1320–50.

Raper, Arthur F. 1933. *The Tragedy of Lynching.* Chapel Hill: University of North Carolina Press.

Reed, Adolph Jr. 1987. "A Critique of Neo–Progressivism in Theorizing about Local Development Policy: A Case from Atlanta." in *The Politics of Urban Development,* ed. Clarence N. Stone and Heywood T. Sanders. Lawrence, KS: The University Press of Kansas.

Reed, John Shelton. 1986. *The Enduring South: Subculture Persistence in Mass Society.* Chapel Hill: University of North Carolina Press.

Reed, John Shelton, and Daniel Joseph Singel, eds. 1982. *Regionalism and the South: Selected Papers of Rupert Vance.* Chapel Hill: University of North Carolina Press.

Ridgway, W. H. 1979. *Community Leadership in Maryland, 1790–1840: A Comparative Analysis of Power in Society.* Chapel Hill: University of North Carolina Press.

Rosdil, Donald L. 1991. "The Context of Radical Populism in US Cities: A Comparative Analysis." *Journal of Urban Affairs* 13:77–96.

Salisbury Daily Times. Salisbury, MD: The Daily Times, Inc.

Schmidt, Steffen W., Laura Guasti, Carl H. Lande, and James C. Scott, eds. 1977. *Friends, Followers, and Factions: A Reader in Political Clientelism.* Berkeley and Los Angeles: University of California Press.

Schultz, Theodore W. 1990. *Restoring Economic Equilibrium: Human Capital in the Modernizing Economy.* Cambridge, MA: Basil Blackwell.

Schumpeter, Joseph A. 1950. *Capitalism, Socialism, and Democracy.* New York: Harper and Row.

Scott, James C. 1976. *The Moral Economy of the Peasant.* New Haven: Yale University Press.

Shor, Ira. 1987. *Critical Teaching and Everyday Life.* Chicago: University of Chicago Press.

———. 1992. *Empowering Education: Critical Teaching for Social Change.* Chicago: University of Chicago Press.

Shor, Ira, and Paulo Freire. *A Pedagogy for Liberatiion: Dialogues on Transforming Education.* New York: Bergin and Garvey.

Smith, Michael P. ed. 1984. *Cities in Transformation*. Urban Affairs Annual Reviews, vol. 26. Beverly Hills: Sage Publications.

Sokolow, Alvin D. 1981. "Local Governments: Capacity and Will." In *Nonmetropolitan America in Transition*, ed. Amos H. Hawley and S. M. Mazie. Chapel Hill: University of North Carolina Press.

Somerset Herald. (1990). March 21. Accomac, Virginia: Atlantic Publications.

Squires, Gregory D., and Thomas A. Lyson. 1987. "Business Incentives, Economic Dislocation and Equal Opportunity: The Impact of Supply–Side Economics on Minority and Female Opportunity." *Journal of Intergroup Relations* 15:29–48.

Staniland, Martin. 1985. *What Is Political Economy?*. New Haven: Yale University Press.

Sternberg, David J. 1981. *How to Complete and Survive a Doctoral Dissertation*. New York: St. Martin's Press.

Sternlieb, George, and James W. Hughes. 1983. *The Atlantic City Gamble*. Cambridge, MA: Harvard University Press.

Stinchcombe, Arthur L. 1968. *Constructing Social Theories*. New York: Harcourt, Brace and World.

Stone, Carl. 1980. *Democracy and Clientelism in Jamaica*. New Brunswick: Transaction Books.

Stone, Clarence N. 1988. "Political Change and Regime Continuity in Postwar Atlanta." Paper prepared for delivery at the annual meeting of the American Political Science Association, the Washington Hilton, Washington, DC, September, 1988.

———. 1989. *Regime Politics: Governing Atlanta 1946–1988*. Lawrence: University Press of Kansas.

———. 1992. "Urban Regimes: A Research Perspective." In *Enduring Tensions in Urban Politic*, ed. Dennis Judd and Paul Kantor. New York: Macmillan.

———. 1993. "Urban Regimes and the Capacity to Govern: A Political Economy Approach." *Journal of Urban Affairs* 15:1–28.

———. 1994. "Group Politics Reexamined: From Pluralism to Political Economy." In *The Dynamics of American Politics: Approaches and Interpretations*, ed. Lawrence C. Dodd and Calvin Jillson. Boulder: Westview Press.

Stone, Clarence N., and Heywood T. Sanders, eds. 1987. *The Politics of Urban Development.* Lawrence: University of Kansas Press.

Summers, Gene F. 1984. "Economic Development and Community Social Change." *Annual Review of Sociology* 10:141–66.

————. 1986. "Rural Community Development." *Annual Review of Sociology* 12:347–71.

Summers, Gene F., ed. 1988. *Agriculture and Beyond: Rural Economic Development.* Proceedings of the Wye Conference, November 9–12, 1987. University of Wisconsin Department of Rural Sociology, Madison.

Swanson, Bert E., Richard A. Cohen, and Edith P. Swanson. 1979. *Small Towns and Small Towners: A Framework for Survival and Growth.* Beverly Hills: Sage Publications.

Swanstrom, Todd. 1985. *The Crisis of Growth Politics.* Philadelphia: Temple University Press.

————. 1988. "Semisoveriegn Cities: The Politics of Urban Development." *Polity* 21:83–110.

————. 1991. "Beyond Economism: Urban Political Economy and the Postmodern Challenge." Paper prepared for the American Political Science Association annual meeting, Washington, DC, August 28 to September 1, 1991.

————. 1993. "Beyond Economism: Urban Political Economy and the Postmodern Challenge." *Journal of Urban Affairs* 15–78.

Touart, Paul Baker. 1990. *Somerset: An Architectural History.* Annapolis: Maryland Historical Trust and Somerset County Historical Trust.

UMES. 1989. Title 9 Economic Adjustment Strategy Grant for Somerset County, Maryland. Princess Anne, University of Maryland Eastern Shore.

U.S. Department of Agriculture (USDA), Economic Research Service. 1987. *Rural Development in the 1980s: Preparing for the Future.* ERS Staff Report No. AGE5870724, Washington, DC.

Vidich, Arthur J., and Joseph Bensman. 1960. *Small Town in Mass Society.* Garden City, New York: Doubleday.

Wallenstein, Peter. 1987. *Slave South to New South: Public Policy in 19th Century Georgia.* Chapel Hill: University of North Carolina Press.

Warner, Sam Bass, Jr. 1968. *The Private City: Philadelphia in Three Periods of Its Growth*. Philadelphia: University of Pennsylvania Press.

Warner, William W. 1987. *Beautiful Swimmers: Watermen, Crabs and the Chesapeake Bay*. New York: Viking Penguin.

Watzlawick, Paul. 1978. *The Language of Change: Elements of Therapeutic Communication*. New York: Basic Books.

Wennersten, John R. 1981. *The Oyster Wars of Chesapeake Bay*. Centreville, MD: Tidewater Publishers.

———. 1992. *Maryland's Eastern Shore: A Journey in Time and Place*. Centreville, MD: Cornell Maritime Press.

———. *Tidewater Somerset: 1850–1970*. Unpublished manuscript.

Whitt, J. Allen. 1982. *Urban Elites and Mass Transportation*. Princeton, NJ: Princeton University Press.

Wiener, Jonathan M. 1978. *Social Origins of the New South: Alabama, 1860–1885*. Baton Rouge: Louisiana State University Press.

Wildavsky, Aaron. 1987. "Choosing Preferences by Constructing Institutions: A Cultural Theory of Preference Fomation." *American Political Science Review* 81:3–21.

Wilson, Thomas C. 1993. "Urbanism and Kinship Bonds: A Test of Four Generalizations." *Social Forces* 71: 703–12.

Wirth, Louis. 1938. "Urbanism as a Way of Life." *American Journal of Sociology*. 44:3–24.

Wolfinger, Raymond E. 1974. *The Politics of Progress*. Englewood Cliffs, N.J.: Prentice-Hall.

Wright, Gavin. 1986. *Old South, New South: Revolutions in the Southern Economy Since the Civil War*. New York: Basic Books.

Zhou, Min. 1992. *Chinatown: The Socioeconomic Potential of an Urban Enclave*. Philadelphia: Temple University Press.

R

DATE DUE